The New Creation
As
Metropolis

Also by Gibson Winter

LOVE AND CONFLICT
THE SUBURBAN CAPTIVITY OF THE CHURCHES

The New Creation
As
Metropolis

BY

GIBSON WINTER

THE MACMILLAN COMPANY
New York

Collier-Macmillan Limited, London

In Gratitude for the Friendship and Example of

C. DANIEL BOONE

and

ROBERT S. TRENBATH

Portions of this book appeared in an article entitled "The New Christendom in the Metropolis" in *Christianity and Crisis*, November 26, 1962.

THE MACMILLAN COMPANY, NEW YORK
COLLIER-MACMILLAN CANADA, LTD., TORONTO, ONTARIO
Divisions of The Crowell-Collier Publishing Company

Library of Congress catalog card number: 63-15703

Printed in the United States of America

Preface

These reflections developed around the problem of mission in the metropolitan areas. The crucial question is whether this mission can be developed from a parochial or congregational base in the residential community. A previous volume had dealt with possibilities of broadening the residential base, but however valid this task for the development of residential chaplaincies to family life, it leaves untouched the vast structures of metropolitan life that determine the shape of our world. This new world of metropolis calls for new forms of the Church if there is to be a mission to the metropolitan world. The nature and form of such a mission are considered in this work.

The concerns of this book will seem somewhat troubling to those who feel that the churches can carry on their mission by doing business as usual. Conviction that the world has not changed in any significant way usually lies back of this hope that the churches may continue in the old paths. But the Church has never continued in an old path when she has been about her true work. To be sure, the Church is the Church only as she lives out of her saving history rather than out of her own instincts or the standards of the world. However, the Church is only the Church as she mediates that saving history in the actual world where she is called to minister. That actual world has never been static and never will be until the end of time. The Church has continually altered her forms of proclamation and ministry as she has borne her witness in the changing situation in the world. Now she is being summoned to radical changes in her forms of apostolate and ministry. Her response to this summons in our time will be the test of her faith and the measure of her apostolicity as the Church.

The author is indebted to the Gray Lectureship of Duke University through whose good offices these reflections were originally presented. He is also appreciative of the opportunity to share one of them with the students and alumni of Berkeley Divinity School under the auspices of the Kingsbury Lecture. Special appreciation is due Dean Robert Cushman and Dean James T. Cleland of Duke University and Dean Richard Wilmer of Berkeley Divinity School, as well as the Pastors Convocation of the Divinity School of Duke University.

GIBSON WINTER

The Divinity School
University of Chicago

CONTENTS

CHAPTER I

The Call to Servanthood

A new society is taking shape before our eyes. This is a society full of promise; it signifies the possibility of life and education on a truly democratic basis. At the same time, the hope of this new society is clouded by the threat of worldwide holocaust, and the promise of its productive power is darkened by alienation between social classes and racial groups. We are experiencing the hope and anxiety that characterize great turning points in history. Only the first few centuries of Christian history, the twelfth century in Western Europe, and perhaps the era of the Reformation can be compared with our own time for critical possibilities. Such periods offer unusual opportunities for

Christian proclamation; by the same token, their potential destructiveness exceeds imagination.

Much of the anxiety generated in such a time arises from confusion about the shape of the world in the making. Amid such confusion societies split between radical conservatism and reckless liberalism—allowing no room for creative development in continuity with social and cultural tradition. This difficulty is, of course, compounded for the churches, since the inherent conservatism of religious institutions casts them too readily in a reactionary role. The task of discerning the world in the making, appraising the divine intention within this process and invoking the claims of the Kingdom in the new society are thus a central work of the Church's mission in our time. The Church cannot preoccupy herself with the maintenance of her own traditions, however important these may be, without simultaneously appraising the situation to which the Christian Message is addressed.

Metropolis

The word "metropolis" identifies this new situation of God's people in the world. Metropolis is the form of the new society; it is emerging out of a welter of conflicting interests. Metropolis is the possibility of a unified, human society arising from the chaos of our massive, urbanized areas. Metropolis is the mother city, the nurturing totality of interdependent regions and municipalities where children may find a climate conducive to growth, where education may enrich life as well as capacities, where men and women may have opportunity to participate as members and receive their rewards, and where advantages may be distributed with equity. Metropolis is the realization of unity of life out of the conflicting factions which now plague metropolitan areas. Metropolis is the fulfillment of the oneness of mankind out of the division of races and classes that now disrupts the metropolitan areas of our country. Metropolis is the human society which different groups subvert and which all groups need for their well-being. Metropolis is the power of the New Mankind refracted through human history.

The unity of human society is a problem in international as well as national contexts. In this respect, metropolis is the local expression of the worldwide search for humanity and life. We could as well, and indeed even more properly, turn our attention to the struggle for an interdependent world out of a background of imperialisms, colonialisms and massive movements of totalitarian organization. However, the international context can be illumined from the task of the Church in metropolis, even as the character of metropolis could be delineated from the international struggle. The elements of the problem are similar, although the concrete expressions vary considerably. No justification need be offered for choosing metropolis over the world as the focus of our reflection. The churches search desperately for their ministry in the large urban areas of our country. They cannot substitute this local responsibility for obligation to the world, and yet their world obligations depend upon their being the Church in this place. Metropolis is the place of this obedience; it is also the form of human society to which this obedience needs to be addressed in this day.

Metropolis serves, therefore, as a criterion with which to evaluate metropolitan development; it is, in this respect, the figure of that unity of life for which we look. The people of the United States, like the people of every industrialized region of the world, are working and living in massive, urban areas which are concentrated around a few major cities. These areas of dense population make up so-called "standard metropolitan areas," but they also blend into strip cities and merge into a kind of megalopolis. These areas are a hodgepodge of interdependent services, diverse school systems and conflicting authorities. To some extent, metropolitan development threatens to devolve into a war of each against all, for every suburban area attempts to zone against large populations which would increase their school expenses and, at the same time, allow for one or two small factories to carry the heavy burden of local taxes. Hence, the metropolis becomes a network of exploitative communities, each vying for tax benefits, each discriminating against classes and races that threaten their autonomy and each contributing to the chaos of spreading blight that now characterizes the metropolitan area. The very notion of metropolis, as the unity

[4]

of the metropolitan region, seems unrealizable in the face of these conflicts between social classes, races and economic interests. Nevertheless, metropolis is the hope for humanity in the midst of this chaos and the figure of the future to which men are summoned.

We need not preoccupy ourselves with the concrete problems of the metropolitan area. This subject is being treated extensively and well in the contemporary literature. Suffice it to say that we verge now on the creation of two cultures in the metropolitan areas: a culture on the periphery which enjoys affluence and privilege; a culture in the central city which suffers discrimination, underemployment and deprivation. Not only is the city failing to realize its promise as a land of freedom and fulfillment, but it is also becoming a breeding ground of social class and racial war that threatens to subvert the total American enterprise. To speak of metropolis, therefore, is to look with hope upon this metropolitan conflict; it is to see the Church in her vocation for humanity. Thus, the notion of metropolis preserves us from the idea that the Church's task is to adjust to contemporary society or to adapt to metropolitan developments. The churches of the past century have adjusted to these urban processes and have come by this route into their captivity to white, middle-class suburbia. The Church lives *in* the metropolitan struggle *for* the unified, interdependent, reconciled society that we call metropolis. The Church is not in the urban area to adapt, but to serve God in the world—to point the world

[5]

toward its fulfillment, to empower it in its realization. The Church is the agency of reconciliation, the witness to metropolis in the midst of metropolitan conflict.

Metropolitan and urban conflict press the churches toward a reconsideration of their nature and task; in fact, we are experiencing an institutional crisis in American Christianity. This crisis appears in almost every aspect of the life of the churches. Pastors, for example, are raising more and more questions about the pastorate—wondering if the proliferation of organizational activity is really an expression of their vocation. Furthermore, an institutional crisis undermines the office of leadership; there is considerable evidence that pastors feel the instability of their position —often manifesting this instability in emotional disturbance. The literature on the inadequacies of organizational Christianity gives further testimony to this crisis, even as recent attempts to renew the congregation indicate an awareness that the successful church may be spiritually empty. The major impact of the metropolitan struggle, however, is to disclose to the churches their isolation from the moving forces of the society, to convince them that they have lost touch with the central dynamic of the society.

The Emerging Role of the Laity

The churches are becoming aware of their isolation in an interesting way; their awakening represents the

The Call to Servanthood

final stage in a long process during which Christianity lost touch with the mainstream of American life. The *emergence of the laity* as the ministering center of Christianity is the creative response of Christianity to this social and cultural estrangement. The institutional crisis may be the moment of birth for a new form of Western Christianity—a new image of the Church—the servanthood of the laity. This new form of the Church can be understood only in the light of the metropolitan struggle and the institutional crisis which it has precipitated.

Massive urbanization changes the relationship of pastors to their communities. A few generations ago, pastors exercised considerable influence on the development of local communities. They were not only in touch with those in positions of power, associating with them as equals in many cases, but they were also aware of personal and social needs in the community. The social services of most American cities in our day are direct outgrowths of special services developed by pastors and churches for their communities. Although the parson was seldom "the person" of the American community, which he was in medieval England, he was, nevertheless, a significant factor in local affairs.

The disruption of this pastoral relationship occurred first in the field of industrial production. The disappearance of paternalistic industry and its replacement by managerial bureaucracy during the twentieth century saw the end of any direct relationship of the

[7]

religious leaders to economic life in the United States.
The Social Gospel movement emerged in protest
against this insulation of Christianity from the productive processes; in fact, the Social Gospel movement was an attempt to establish a new type of pastorate to economic life. The failure of the Social
Gospel to discriminate between the Kingdom of God
and a redeemed economy caused the next generation
to reject the profound truth of this protest along with
its theological error.

The churches now find the residential communities—the very centers in which the churches have
maintained their congregational communities—undergoing a technological transformation similar to the
Industrial Revolution. The churches hoped that the
autonomy of economic life could be overcome through
the personal influence of Christians. However illusory,
this view fitted the American religious pattern. New
residential communities are also moving beyond the
Church's ken or control. The day of direct intervention by pastors in community life is rapidly disappear-
ing except in the smaller towns. Metropolitan areas
are developing through a conflict of economic interests and through the coordination of such interests
in urban planning and political compromise. The
churches participate in these processes only to the
degree that sensitive laymen raise questions in planning councils and political boards. However, such in-
stances are all too rare both because laymen have been
made to think that Christianity concerns events within

[8]

the religious establishments and because laymen have been given little or no help in discerning the theological dimensions of community development.

The present transformation in residential community is similar to that which occurred in economic life at the turn of the century. The processes of human organization are so complex under technological conditions that economic production has to be planned; similarly a technologically organized metropolis has to be planned. In economic life, responsibility for organization was gradually invested in skilled managements who became relatively independent even of their stockholders. Planners of metropolitan development are in principle much more accessible to social and political control and are, therefore, not nearly so insulated from religious organizations; nevertheless, metropolitan development has become so complex that planning has become rather technical, and even urban planners lack adequate understanding of the effects of their schemes upon human values and personal life. Hence, denominations find changes occurring in the residential communities at a much faster pace than they can follow, and religious professionals are baffled by the technical complexity of the planning that is necessary for realizing a more human metropolis. The direct influence of pastors upon community development becomes more and more difficult; consequently the influence of Christianity on the residential environment in coming generations will have to be the work of laity who are familiar with the

[9]

technical problems and engaged in the planning processes.

The insulation of religious activities from social and cultural structures in a technological society is not confined to economic and residential life. A similar process occurred in the colleges and universities after the middle of the nineteenth century. Perhaps scientific technology and military development provide the most dramatic examples of the emergence of a technological élite who are inaccessible to the religious establishments. Science and technology made possible a large, complex society; simultaneously they gave rise to echelons of technicians who make decisions and administer the various structures of the society. The residential structure is only one among many spheres of such technological organization, but it impinges directly upon the religious establishments, because it provides the locus of congregational and parochial organization. To this extent, the metropolitan struggle has brought to light the gradual alienation of religious institutions from the centers of power in modern mass society. A laity who participate in the processes of society and develop theological sensitivity form the only possible Church in a mass society. This is as true in economic and military life as it is in metropolitan organization. However, the churches hesitate before this task of encouraging a ministering laity, for they cherish their traditional patterns of ministry.

If the Church as responsible laity is the only Church that can minister to a technological society, then the clericalized church of the active pastor and passive laity may give all the outward signs of being a church but it is not participant in the world and, in this respect, is not God's people in the world. Metropolis, as a complex process of planned interdependence of life, is evoking a new form of the Church—the servanthood of the laity.

This is not to suggest that religious professionals can ignore the forces that are shaping our communal life. Pastors and other religious professionals should gain far more understanding of technological society than they have at present, if they are to fulfill their task in relation to the servanthood of the laity. However, a religious professional cannot and should not hope to be expert in these fields. Contemporary society is much too complex in its organization and processes to be subject to direct guidance by religious professionals. By the same token, this society is much too diversified in its structures to allow for a simple unification of life through a Christian congregation within a residential community. Indeed, residential community itself depends upon complex metropolitan processes to shape its values, even as the small town is dominated by the mass society. A laity, theologically self-conscious and socially alert, is the form through which the Church's witness in metropolitan society will be realized. Metropolis itself is calling forth this form of the Church, for the struggle for metropolitan unity is also the struggle for a human society. Metropolis and Christianity are distinct historical realities, but they are inextricably interwoven in the metropolitan struggle.

Pietism or Servanthood

The culture of the churches is antithetical to the Church as servanthood of the laity. Perhaps this is why the lay movement has failed to materialize in the United States since World War II. American Christianity derives its cultural expression from the residential milieu; consequently to understand the culture of the churches one has to understand this residential environment.

The residential community is preoccupied with the maintenance of emotional stability and the nurture of children. These are its principal interests; significant aspects of life, indeed, but they do not exhaust the values of personality and society. Moreover, familial and residential community counterbalances tensions generated in other sectors of the society; by the same token, these communities are no longer a dynamic source of social development. Residential associations are now insulated associations serving to reduce social tensions; for this reason, it is extremely difficult to achieve racial or social class integration in a residential setting. Even access to residential community is contingent upon position in the economic apparatus; the housing to which one may have access and consequently the human associations to which one may belong are determined largely by occupational achievement. Residential community and its values are determined by the dynamics of an industrial society. Churches that organize their existence around residential communities likewise become reflectors of economic and technological forces. A religious establishment in a residential community becomes an adjustive rather than a creative force in a technical society.

The churches today are indeed preoccupied with the private values of emotional balance and the nurture of children, even as one would expect in view of the residential culture in which the churches are rooted. This preoccupation is attested most dramatically by the strange coalition which has arisen between the denominational churches and Billy Graham's evangelistic crusades. On the surface, it seems very natural that the denominations should cooperate with Billy Graham in his crusades. Both movements are concerned with spreading the Gospel. Anything that furthers the cause of Christianity should occasion a pooling of efforts. However, the coalition of denominational Christianity and the Gospel tent is a rather recent phenomenon. The denominations have generally been sympathetic with revivalism and have even encouraged this tradition of evangelism, but recently the denominations have sponsored the Billy Graham crusades as integral to their work in the large metropolitan areas. Indeed, the denominations have attempted to exploit Billy Graham's wide appeal in the cities to further the work of the churches. They have turned to the tradition of individual conversion in order to pour vitality into the organization churches of the metropolitan areas. The new phenomenon is not sympathy between the denominations and revivalism but rather the tendency of the denominations to see the tradition of individualistic evangelism as their task. There are, of course, differences among the denominations with respect to their traditional affinities with individualistic evangelism, but these differences seem to have disappeared since World War II; Lutheran and Episcopal churches participate in the Graham crusades as readily as Methodist and Baptist.

The coalition of denominational Christianity and revivalism is founded upon a shared preoccupation with private or individual values. This is the common ground that unites the organization church with the evangelistic tent. Hence, denominational churches no longer feel the inadequacies of the highly individualistic and subjective emphases of revivalism. Billy Graham, of course, makes no apology for his conviction that the crucial work of evangelism is to bring the individual to a decision for Christ. This is evangelism as Billy Graham understands it, and, indeed, he stands very much within the tradition of revivalism on this point. The churches, by contrast, have traditionally understood subjective faith and experience in the context of the sacraments, true teaching and the ministry of proclamation. The churches have traditionally recognized the subjective aspects of belief and experience, but they have set these aspects in relation to the objective reality of the Word in Scripture, Sacrament and Church. Moreover, the churches of the Reformation have never viewed the conversion of individuals as an adequate resolution of the social responsibility of Christianity. There were, to be sure, pietistic trends in most of the denominations and periods during which individual conversion seemed to be a total expression of the Gospel, but these pietistic strands were partial rather than exhaustive realizations of the Reformation traditions.

The Gospel tent is not merely limited or incomplete, therefore, in its exclusive stress on individual conversion and subjective decision. In the light of the Reformation traditions, the Gospel tent is a distortion of Christianity, for it isolates individual decision from the total context of proclamation and pure teaching in which it receives its authentic grounding and continuity. To say this, of course, is to focus on the mainstream of the Reformation, for the left wing of the Reformation stressed individual conversion and subjective experience. Revivalism has roots in this left wing of the Reformation, although it lacks the sense of corporate discipline which characterized sectarian movements like Anabaptism.

Reinhold Niebuhr drew attention to the cleavage between the denomination and revivalism during the Graham crusade in New York City. He received many letters of criticism from Lutherans for questioning the relationship between Billy Graham's work and the task of the denominations. His comment upon receiving these letters was interesting; he remarked that pietism was still very powerful in American Lutheranism, in fact much more powerful as a force than he had imagined. Here is the common ground between Billy Graham and the denominations in post-World War II America: both are committed to a pietistic understanding of Christianity, where pietism means a reduction of Christianity to subjective feelings.

Billy Graham comes to pietism by the direct path of conviction, for this is his basic understanding of Christianity. Christianity for the Gospel tent is condensed in the personal experience of conversion to Christ. All the rest flows from this: the authenticity of the preaching is not tested by tradition or apostolic symbol but by its power to evoke such personal decisions; the validity of the Church's life does not rest upon its unity, holiness, apostolicity but upon the presence in its midst of those who have made decisions and had experiences; the task of the churches in society is not defined with reference to the redemption of creation amidst the ambiguities of sin, for the health of society is an inevitable effect flowing from the presence of "converted" individuals. Revivalism is an American expression of pietism; Billy Graham is one of its leading exponents and the denominations have joined his camp.

The denominations come by their pietism through the pietistic currents in American Christianity but also through the private character of the concerns of the residential communities in which they assemble. The

[16]

residential community is a consumer's world, set apart from the productive world both by distance and social climate. The concerns of technological production are shut out from the residential community, at least in the American ideal of the suburban development. This consumer world has a special morality of exclusiveness that taboos the mixing of racial or social class groups in the residential milieu. Family, home, children, local church, local school and local politics form the horizon of interests that preoccupy the residential community. These highly individualistic values have become the dominant themes of denominational religious life. Thus, by virtue of its residential milieu the denominational church concentrates upon the subjective concerns which are promulgated by the Gospel tent. The denominational churches were transmuted to pietism by their residential milieu. Having undergone this transformation, they see no difficulty in making common cause with revivalism.

Once the metropolitan struggle is taken seriously and one realizes that the creation of metropolis calls for a servanthood of the laity, the Graham crusade and its denominational support can be evaluated in its true light. These crusades divert Christians from the real task of the Church in the metropolis. They distort the Gospel, the Church and the character of the struggle to which the churches are summoned. The Graham crusade fosters pietism in place of servanthood. The Graham crusade uses the techniques of mass society to perpetuate the individualistic piety of the frontier

[17]

town, whereas the role of the Church in the metropolis is to discern and proclaim the meaning of the struggle for a human society. At the moment when a crisis of public responsibility undermines metropolitan development, the denominations join forces with the Graham crusade to foster the notion that private experiences are the heart of the Christian message. Pietism replaces servanthood in the moment of metropolitan crisis, disillusioning those who had looked to the churches for some direction in this hour of social class and racial conflict, encouraging those who stand to profit from the exploitation of the central city.

To be sure, some denominational leaders have opposed this coalition of the churches with the Graham crusade. Nevertheless, the denominations have lacked theological understanding on which to oppose the coalition with the Gospel tent, for the leaders of these denominations are largely concerned with the organizational expansion of the churches in residential areas. They do not see the Graham crusade as a diversion from this organizational expansion in suburbia, because the private values of suburbia are fostered by the Graham crusade, if in a somewhat exaggerated way. Consequently, even the denominational opposition to the coalition has been rather half-hearted. The denominations see the metropolis through the lens of suburban residential communities. They do not conceive their responsibility as ministering to the total metropolitan area, witnessing to its destiny as a human society and an interdependent metropolis. They see their task as building, building, building—worship centers, Sunday school quarters and meeting halls for organizations in every new residential area. They call this "churching" new residential areas. Therefore, any publicity in favor of private values, whether by Billy Graham or anyone else, seems to help their cause. Once the task of the churches is really understood, however, and the problem of cultivating a ministering laity in centers of public responsibility becomes the essential task, then the Graham crusade is seen for what it really is—a pietistic diversion of energies and resources which only confuses Christians and non-Christians as to the meaning of the Gospel, the nature of the Church and the task of Christianity in the metropolitan area.

This interpretation of the Graham crusade is not made with a view to disparaging the enterprise in which Billy Graham is engaged. He is a representative of the revivalist tradition in modern guise. His work, even as the work of Billy Sunday and many others, may have validity within its own tradition. His work is not the work of the churches, and the denominations subvert their own vocation when they attempt to exploit Billy Graham for publicity. Denominational confusion over this issue can be understood in the light of the private, subjective values which dominate the residential milieu of the denominational churches, but this understanding does not excuse the lack of vision and theological depth which have led the denominations to forsake their real task in the metropolitan area. They are using techniques of mass society to foster their organizational interests when these very techniques need to be used in a responsible way for the creation of a human environment.

The Role of Piety in Christian Mission

The Church as servant, the servanthood of the laity as the Church, and other similar terms need to receive much fuller treatment in subsequent discussions, since these are the terms which have been contrasted with pietism and subjective experiences. However, there is a qualification with respect to pietistic values that needs to be made in the present context. Every image of the Church involves an appropriate kind of piety, a corresponding personal devotion and exercise in the Christian life. This subjective side of the historical existence of the Church is integral to Christianity; indeed, personal devotion and discipline have always played a significant part in the total life and witness of the churches.

When servanthood is contrasted with pietism in the present day, the contrast is between churches that are engaged in the metropolitan struggle through witnessing laity and churches that are insulated from the public struggle and preoccupied with the private values of residential community. There will be a piety appropriate to the servanthood of the laity in the metropolis, but it will be a very different kind of piety from that of the medieval churches or the frontier towns. The piety of the churches in residential communities is really the piety of the frontier projected upon a metropolitan world.

The piety of medieval Europe developed in the context of a feudal society under the hierarchy of the church. No society is ever static, and yet the serfs, knights, lords, clergy and others had obligations and rights which were rather well established; movement between these positions was highly restricted. Within each of these functions, certain kinds of personal devotion and piety were appropriate; moreover, the exercise of such piety contributed to the total well-being and ultimate salvation of all. Not too much was expected of the serf beyond certain sacramental duties and reverence. Knights were expected to maintain certain standards of virtue and valor, charity and sacrifice. Lords were given license in certain phases of life such as sexuality, exploitation and pillage, but in turn were expected to support the religious institutions and protect the religious enterprise. Within the religious hierarchy as well there developed appropriate levels of piety: those with "vocations" increased the treasury of merit through their disciplined lives; parish priests observed a minimal piety and implemented the sacramental system and discipline of the church. Despite its great variety and the number of enthusiastic movements which swept medieval Europe, particularly in periods of crisis like that of the Black Death, a hierarchy of appropriate kinds of piety emerged in support of the organic unity of that society—a hierarchy expressing the ultimate coherence of the society in its orientation toward the vision of God.

Our own traditions of piety root much more directly in the pietistic movements of the Reformation than in the contemplative piety of medieval Europe. When one considers the social concern and practical charity that issued from the movements of Spener, Franke and the Methodist Revival, it is quite evident that pietistic concern with the experiences of faith need not degenerate into the private preoccupations of pietism. The Methodist movement in England is perhaps the most decisive example of the social significance of a piety which was appropriate to a particular form of the Church in a specific social situation. The working classes had entered English cities in search of work as they were closed off the land. They were "pewed out" of the churches, as E. C. Wickham so vividly expressed it in his book, *Church and People in an Industrial City;* that is to say, the spatial allotments in the Anglican churches provided for only the upper estates and the wealthier middle classes. The laboring poor were simply excluded from the common worship of the English people. Moreover, the conditions of the working classes during these centuries following the Reformation were worse than anything experienced in the horrors of nineteenth century America. The ministry of reconciliation exercised through the Methodist revival remains a landmark of mission and social concern in the history of the Christian Church. Here the piety of the Protestant Church is manifest in the context of a vital, sacrificial mission; indeed, a similar story can be told for the pietistic movements of Germany and Scandinavia. It is not simply the stress on subjective experience which converts an appropriate piety into pietism but the removal of this subjective emphasis from the missionary witness of the churches in the whole field of human life. The private concerns of the residential milieu have transmuted the piety of an earlier period into an escape from public responsibility and Christian mission.

The United States has had its own tradition of piety, emerging from the struggle to shape the American continent into a field for freedom and prosperity. Various strands of this piety inform the denominational and sectarian churches to this day, although certain aspects become less prominent with each passing generation. This American piety is usually called Puritan by its enemies, although it has no closer connection with Puritanism than it does with the Methodism of the frontier and the disciplined virtues of the Bible belt. This piety is broadly comparable to the virtues of the Protestant ethic as Max Weber depicted them; it represents one expression of Christianity in the context of an emerging industrial society. The striking contrast to medieval piety is found in the universal application of this piety to all members of the society. One kind of devotion, personal conviction and integrity is expected of all. Clergy and laity alike are expected to abstain from pleasures that smack of indulgence. Alcoholic beverages are looked at askance, and even those who indulge feel constrained to justify their indulgence. Many aspects of life are subjected to close scrutiny, ranging from private values such as frugality and diligence in work to avoidance of pleasure for its own sake and preservation of sexual and moral purity. This piety crystallized a set of subjective attitudes which confirmed one's rightness with God and preserved one's relationship with the church. Since each man had to do his own believing and each would be saved through his own faith and righteousness, no organic hierarchy of functions could provide salvation through a treasury of merit. Piety had a highly individualistic and extremely moral character—perhaps even legalistic—and yet it applied to all and produced a society in which honesty and rigorous discipline helped to preserve life and tame the wilderness.

The individualistic emphasis in American piety has become less and less appropriate to the problems of the metropolitan context; this piety fails to express the authentic impulses of the redemptive community in its ministry to the metropolitan area. Many religious groups preserve the virtues of nineteenth century piety in the private, residential contexts of suburbia, using this piety to rationalize their rejection of public responsibility for the metropolis and their exclusion of other racial groups. Indeed, the private values of traditional American piety perpetuate reactionary forces in our day when the resolution of many problems must come about through corporate organization of life on a metropolitan scale. For example, the virtues of self-reliance which were so appropriate to the frontier situation are now used to advocate right-to-work laws that are damaging to the interests of unskilled workers. The frontier emphasis on thrift and independence is used as an argument against social provision of medical care in a technological age when medical care requires costly facilities and preserves life at a cost far beyond the financial resources of any but the richest people. Thus, traditional piety becomes a means of subverting the Gospel and its responsibilities, turning men and women away from their calling to mission and justifying their neglect of the imperatives of love in a new situation. The piety of an individualistic frontier subverts the Gospel in an emerging metropolis.

To defend piety as an important aspect of the Church's life is not to propose that our immediate task is to cultivate a piety appropriate to metropolis. This is the mistake of most of the renewal movements in the churches. True piety emerges in the engagement of the Church with the world. *True piety is the subjective expression of the objective ministry of the Church in the world*. Only as the churches become the servanthood of the laity in the metropolitan areas will a piety emerge which is appropriate to metropolis. The Christian style of life is not the means to engagement in the world but the consequence of a ministry in the world. Christian virtues and perspectives enter into every ministry, of course, but the task of the Church can never be understood as the cultivation of such subjective attitudes and virtues. The Church is in the world to proclaim to the world its place within the saving history, man's history with God. The Church is not in the world to cultivate the emotional and moral integrity of its membership. The Church is not a spiritual culture society nor is it an ethical culture society, despite the appropriation of this name by one of the liberal churches of our day. The Church proclaims and lives a message of deliverance, freedom and hope in a world which finds itself caught in bondage and hopelessness. In that ministry and witness, Christians and the Christian Church manifest a piety, devotion, consecration and commitment which are appropriate to their witness in that particular moment of history. One can look for a new style of piety as the servanthood of the laity becomes the ministering reality of the Christian Church. However, every attempt to cultivate piety among the laity in preparation for such a ministry diverts this development, for it turns attention once again to the private values which contradict the servanthood of the laity in the world of metropolis. Nothing more can or should be said about the piety appropriate to the ministering servant in metropolis beyond his openness to God's gracious presence and his commitment to God's reconciling ministry in the public realm.

To be sure, moral virtues take their place in sustaining the relationships among men in society. Sexual purity, personal honesty and many other virtues have as much currency in metropolis as they had in medieval Europe or frontier America. However, certain styles of life and certain virtues stand out in particular periods of the Church's life and witness. Consider, for example, the virtues peculiar to the Christian resistance under Hitler: self-control, patience, fearlessness, resistance to pain, and many other special qualities of life. Particular virtues and attitudes, appropriate to a world and ministry of the Church, are invested with a special quality as the subjective side of that ministry and witness. In this sense one can understand the continuing appropriateness of many of the values ensconced in the piety of the American frontier, while still recognizing that these private values may not express the prominent features of a piety appropriate to the servanthood of the laity. When one contrasts pietism with servanthood in our day, therefore, one projects an opposition between a piety that is rooted in the individualistic values appropriate to the frontier and the public responsibility of servanthood which is called for in the metropolitan struggle. The calling of the Church in metropolis is obscured whenever appeal is made to this frontier piety.

The Institutional Crisis

The institutional crisis of Christianity in the United States can be understood in the light of this contrast between pietism and servanthood. The organization, worship, ministry and teaching of the churches perpetuate the private values of pietism so congenial to residential life. The struggle in the metropolitan area calls for public responsibility, coherent ministries to the whole metropolis, and the servanthood of the laity in the public spheres. Many pastors and laymen feel that their religious activities divert their attention from public responsibility in the metropolitan struggle, and yet the pietism of the organization church seems to be the only option for religious practice. Indeed, the depth of this crisis is confirmed by the detachment of church people from even the most rudimentary grasp of the meaning of the Christian faith. Despite enormous expenditures of money, a well trained clergy, modern religious paraphernalia and high-powered mimeograph machines, the churches have failed to communicate a Christian understanding of life in the American community.

Pastors confront this poverty of Christian understanding at every hospital bed and during almost every bereavement. Those who have devoted time and energy to religious activity, and this applies to pastors as well as laity, discover in the crises of sickness and bereavement that there is no discernible relation between the Gospel and their predicament. The Gospel has not penetrated the world of science and nature in which their lives are being lived. The Gospel is not really integral to the technological world by which their lives have been conditioned. The religious life of the churches has been a kind of make-believe in which a traditional piety and traditional forms of worship and preaching seemed to give security and sanction. In the moment of crisis, the gap between the world in which they were really living and the religious institution opened into a yawning chasm. The meaning of prayer, the character of death, the reality of sin and the truth of redemption somehow escaped them, even though they had given outward acknowledgment to the traditional piety. The profound guilt over broken relationships in work, perfidy in their personal history and adultery in their ideal marriages remained outside the purview of this piety. In the crisis of sickness, unemployment or bereavement, these betrayals and perfidies flood in upon the person, revealing the emptiness of the traditional religious practice.

Furthermore, pastors experience estrangement from the forces that are disrupting the lives of those to whom they minister. The residential community in which most pastorates are exercised is no longer the dynamic center of society. Home is the place for licking one's wounds, finding refuge in personal relationships and enjoying a certain leisure. Residence and family life *react to* the dynamics of society, suffering anxieties that are engendered in the productive process. Moreover, the strains of industrial production are such that pastors deal with widespread emotional disturbance in these residential communities without access to the sources of these disturbances. They deal with the symptoms: broken homes, disturbed personalities and delinquent children. The load of personal, pastoral care increases day by day, but the forces that create these problems become daily more remote from the pastor in the residential community. The pastor ministers in a sanitarium, treating the shock cases but never discovering the enemy who is inflicting the damage.

The institutional crisis of Christianity arises, thus, from the preoccupation of the religious community with private concerns while the forces that are shaping human destiny dominate the public realm. Pastors feel this estrangement in their own isolation from the processes of the society—their sense of working in a hothouse atmosphere of women's emotional difficulties and children's programs. Laity experience this crisis in a search for a significant ministry in place of the organizational activities to which the churches usually consign their efforts. Religious leaders sense the depth of this crisis at the very moment when they press for organizational expansion, since the proliferation of residential churches seems to have so little impact on the increasing chaos of the metropolitan areas. The institutional crisis of contemporary Christianity is manifest in the simultaneous appearance of spiritual emptiness and intense religious activity. The crisis is generated by a situation calling for a servant Church over against a denominational commitment to pietism.

The institutional crisis in Christianity is erroneously attributed simply to institutionalism. The pietistic tradition of the United States penetrates deeply into the American religious consciousness and fosters the notion that pure religion is formless and spiritual, implying that religion is corrupted by formal ministries, rites and organization. Hence, the institutional crisis

[30]

is often attributed to the growth of denominational bureaucracies and religious organizations. Two remedies are suggested for this excessive institutionalism: on the one hand, spiritual inspiration of the kind that Billy Graham represents is recommended to enliven the dry bones; on the other hand, mobilizing lay manpower to take a more active part in things is suggested as a way of adding vitality to the machinery. Clearly, the inspirational approach of the Graham variety only deepens the institutional crisis, since it widens the chasm between metropolitan problems and religious preoccupation with the nurture of personal needs. Tapping the great resource of lay manpower has proved again and again since World War II to be a way of siphoning off the servanthood of the laity into irrelevant activities around the religious establishment. In both cases, the institutional crisis is misunderstood and the remedy only aggravates the sickness.

The institutional crisis of Christianity is symptomatic of a rejection of ministry by the churches. The consequence of this rejection is a loss of substance in the religious enterprise. Institutions have a twofold relationship to the religious reality: they proclaim a relationship to the ground of being, the source of all reality; moreover, they embody a ministry in service of the ultimate reality, mediating the presence of that which they proclaim. Religious institutions go through crises during the breakdown of either one or both of these relationships, either failing to elicit faith because they obscure rather than proclaim the Gospel, or ob-

[31]

structing presence by refusal of ministry. The Reformation came about as a consequence of an institutional crisis in proclamation; the performance of rites was separated from anchorage in faith—a shadow of presence replaced the substance of hope. The present crisis has arisen through the diversion of Christian faith from servanthood into preoccupation with a private relationship of faith—the Reformation concern with faith is emptied of the substance of ministry. Either type of institutional crisis is bound to react upon the other, of course; as the Reformation brought a renewal of ministry even so the modern crisis calls for a new mode of proclamation. However, the occasions of the crises are different and the focus of renewal will consequently be different. In the metropolitan crisis, the breakdown of obedience and ministry is the cause for the emptying of spiritual substance from the religious enterprise; thus, the appearance of a servanthood of the laity will be the focus of renewal of the churches. The churches now face a decision between pietism which serves as an obstacle to ministry and servanthood of the laity which will bring a radical transformation in the whole character of religious life.

The servanthood of the laity involves a different conception of the relationship of the Church to the world from that which is current in the United States. Many religious leaders do not feel any particular obligation to consider metropolis as a field of mission, for they believe that the ministry of the churches should be carried on within the religious establishment by men who have been especially trained for a clergyman's work. Metropolis and the struggles for a human world would presumably take care of themselves when and if enough people enjoyed the ministrations of the religious establishment. Thus, the work of the church is to increase its nominal membership and minister faithfully to those within its walls through the best professional ministry that is available. When one speaks of a servanthood of the laity, not as a nice addition to round out a professional ministry but as *the* ministry of the Church, then a wholly different conception of the relationship of Church to world has been introduced.

The underlying thesis of these considerations is that the world is radically changed; a wholly new relationship of Church to world is called for in our time. This new relationship can be described as the servanthood of the laity. Here indeed we encounter the real division among Christians today: one group feels that the world has not changed in any fundamental sense and that the churches should go about their work as usual; the other group is convinced that the contemporary world has a new universe of meaning, a radically different social structure and problems peculiar to its own time. If one sides with the former group, the churches need only do better what they have been doing. If one sides with those who claim that the contemporary world is radically different in most major respects, then one is open to consider the servanthood of the laity in this new society.

CHAPTER II

The Servant Church
in a Secularized World

The terms "secular" and "secularization" have a negative connotation for religious people. For example, one often reads in popular religious literature that Christian forces should join to combat secular forces. Indeed, godless materialism and secular forces are often treated as synonymous. Hence, the notion that secularization is a consequence of the Gospel strikes religious people as a bit nonsensical. However, the term "secular" is too valuable to be discarded without a struggle; at least, the universe that lies behind the notion of the secular needs to be identified and understood, for it is the universe of the twentieth century and the universe within which the Church is called to minister.

Secularization of the World

The term secularization was first used as a neutral word to designate the expropriation of church lands for distribution to various principalities in the Treaty of Westphalia (1648). The Thirty Years War had created problems of indemnities as well as bitter feelings. The attempt to settle these conflicts at Westphalia led to the partition of lands, which had traditionally been administered by the Archbishopric of Bremen and the Bishopric of Verdun, to some of the competing principalities as compensation. The diplomatic problems created in this transfer of lands called for a neutral term to soften the blow to the churches. The term "secular" had always meant worldly in the neutral or even good sense, as for example in the contrast between parish priests who lived in the world (secular) and the priests in monastic orders (regular) who lived according to a rule outside the world. Worldly or secular, thus, had no derogatory connotations but only implied a difference in sphere of obligations. Hence, the use of the term "secularization" for the partition of lands at the Treaty of Westphalia only implied a transfer of administration from the spiritual kingdom to the temporal kingdom.

The notion of secular refers to a sphere of work in

the world, and secularization means a shift of responsibility from religious authority to worldly authority. Both terms suggest a loss of administrative control by the church, but this loss of direct administrative control never implied godlessness. To be sure, secularized lands might be administered by godless principalities who exploited them, but the same can be said of lands which were administered by religious authorities in medieval Europe solely for the benefit of avaricious bishops. There is no principle by which secularization need lead to godlessness any more than administration by religious authorities would have to lead to godly and just administration. This applies as well in the twentieth century as in the twelfth; for example, the pay scale and working conditions in religious establishments in the United States are notoriously unjust by the standards of compensation and work in industry.

Administration by religious authorities was founded in a view of the universe rather than in the exercise of a principle of justice, and it is the collapse of this world view which paved the way for secularization. In the medieval world view, the church administered the salvation of mankind through the distribution of sacramental grace, by proper instruction in the right beliefs, by persecution of error and by preservation of the social order. The church possessed revealed knowledge of the final end of man and controlled the essential means to this end; the laity served as the administrative arm of the religious hierarchy in preserving mankind for its transcendent goal. Thus, the church

[36]

shared administrative responsibility with temporal authorities and interpreted this as a delegation of power to nobles and princes by the religious authority. This was the crucial significance of the mythical Donation of Constantine by which all authority in the West was handed over to the religious authority. On the basis of this Donation, all authority rested with the hierarchy which delegated this authority to princes in order to bring all Christendom under God's rule and preserve it for its salvation. Thus the priority of the spiritual kingdom was established; the institution responsible for man's final end set the guidelines for the fulfillment of preliminary ends.

The old Christendom or medieval Christendom embraced the notion, therefore, of a kingdom of mankind under the direction of a religious authority which possessed the truth and controlled man's access to his destiny. The laity fulfilled certain administrative tasks under this religious or priestly authority. They formed a temporal, administrative arm of the hierarchy, carrying out such duties as the religious authority allocated to them. For example, the temporal arm, or laity, had responsibility for the execution of heretics, although the religious authority controlled the judgment of heretics. To be sure, this understanding of the laity as administrative arm of the hierarchy was seldom perfectly realized in practice, for the worldly powers contested such power in the church from the very first; but medieval Christendom found its unity in man's heavenly destiny and gave worldly expression to this unity through the authority of the hierarchy and the administrative work of its lay arm.

Secularization came about with the recognition that the ordering of life fell to mankind under God and not by delegation from the religious hierarchy. Secularization represents the collapse of ecclesiastical totalitarianism. The initial break in the old Christendom came with the Reformation, for the Lutheran and Calvinist movements in different ways rejected the medieval notion of the Church's sole authority over the whole of life. Luther's conception of the two kingdoms, however troublesome it may have become in later developments, was essentially an attack upon the old Christendom and upon the sole authority of the papal hierarchy in the direction of the world. For Luther, the kingdom of the left hand, or the temporal kingdom, exercised its authority as a kind of mask or indirect expression of the authority and wrath of God, restraining men from sin and preserving their lives from destruction. Luther did not think of this temporal kingdom as godless but considered it as ruled by divinely bestowed reason according to a rough sense of justice. God entrusted this work of justice to men in their vocations in the world. Hence, Luther encouraged a process of secularization or freeing of mankind for responsibility under God in relative independence of the religious authority. This is a first step toward secularization; it breaks the domination of the hierarchy in order to purify the spiritual kingdom, thus creating two worlds where there had been one.

However, Luther chained the temporal kingdom to the orders of creation—the structures of a traditional society which were now withdrawn from the hegemony of the religious hierarchy.

John Calvin encouraged a process of secularization of a different kind but with much the same effect. He conceived of the magistrate or worldly authority as implementing God's law in the community for the preservation of life and the fulfillment of God's will for mankind in the world. The discipline of the Geneva community was not exercised by a religious authority but was vested in the public authority and influenced by the religious leaders. The domination of the religious hierarchy was broken by the Calvinist recognition of worldly authority under God. The church exercised its influence in political life by preaching and teaching. The laity became God's vicegerents for the Law.

The old Christendom collapsed under the blows of the Reformation; indeed the unity of Christendom had been largely mythical; the Eastern church had broken its relationship with the papacy long before, but the hierarchy had been able to perpetuate a myth of universal domination in the foreshortened landscape of medieval Europe. The emergence of nation states, the opening of geographical horizons after the Crusades, the influx of wealth from the New World, the rediscovery of classical learning through contact with the Arabic world, and many other factors led to the collapse of Christendom and the beginning of secularization. However, the Protestant movements crystallized the initial step of secularization and reinforced its development in the emerging nation states. Man began to assume responsibility for his history and for the pursuit of truth.

We are not concerned with the development of secularization except as it sheds light on the contemporary ministry of the Church. Hence, we can pass over much of the detail of the struggle of the Catholic Counter-Reformation to restore the myth of European unity against the nascent forces of a new world. The struggle against scientific development by the religious hierarchy, as for example in the attacks on Galileo and Copernicus, were shared in time by the Protestant churches, for the opening of the universe to rational speculation and reflection seemed to threaten the religious view of man's universe. Secularization came slowly in both Protestant and Catholic worlds. The break in medieval Christendom was not yet a recognition of man's responsibility in history. Indeed, the secularization of political authority during the Reformation can be understood largely from the reformers' need to strengthen their hand with political allies against domination by the papal authority.

Secularization issued from the separation of political and social authorities from the religious establishment. How, then, can such a process be described as a consequence of Christianity in the West? Is not secularization merely symptomatic of the gradual dissolution of

Christianity in the West—a process which is only reaching its final stages in the twentieth century?

There is no question that the Western world has won its secularization through a running battle with the churches. However, the ground for this worldly authority is essentially Christian, even though the churches have not always recognized or acknowledged this ground. Luther and Calvin were on sound theological ground when they recognized the authority of the worldly, political powers under God. They undoubtedly reflected on this true character of political authority because they had to contend with the political domination of the Roman hierarchy, but their understanding of worldly responsibility was grounded in their recognition of the salvation of man by faith through grace. Their recognition of this principle undercut the whole notion of a religious establishment which could arrogate to itself control over the means to salvation. No political, social, cultural or religious form could claim absolute truth against the twofold recognition of God's absolute sovereignty and His gracious gift of salvation in Jesus Christ. Any structure of the world, including the religious structure, which arrogated to itself the authority to dispense this salvation through works which it controlled, whether religious or political, fell directly under the judgment of this Reformation doctrine. That churches of the Reformation tradition did not always acknowledge their own theological ground goes without saying, but the ground had been laid in the Reformation for a secularization of life in the West. If the religious institution also had to be justified by faith through grace, then religious institutions were ranged along with others under the judgment and grace of God. Man had passed from the tutelage of medieval Christendom, from his childhood under a religious authority, to a new world of responsibility before God.

Man's openness to his history before God poses all kinds of threats to religious institutions, for faith becomes trust in God and commitment to His work in history rather than loyalty to a religious organization. The churches not only face the problem of understanding and encouraging a secularization which poses threats to traditional religious structures, but they also bear the burden of delivering mankind from its fear of freedom and responsibility.

The churches face the task of secularizing their own institutions. Dietrich Bonhoeffer was pointing to this task when he referred to the need for a religionless Christianity; that is, the recognition of man's struggle for a human world as the sphere of the decisions of faith. Recent attempts to secularize the Gospel are similarly struggling with this task of secularization within the institutional and theological structures of Christianity itself, for the logical consequence of secularization is the recognition of the Church as part of history. If secularization is the true character of the world as *free for responsibility* before God, then we can understand the need for secularization within the religious institutions, for they are the witnesses to this deliverance of man for responsibility.

The Nature of Secularism

Secularism or idolatry in religion is denial of the historical character of religious institutions, attributing to their forms a changeless, nonhistorical status. Thus, secularism is a rejection of secularization in the churches or in the world; it is a denial of the creaturely, changing character of all historical reality. Where secularization is the deliverance of mankind from bondage to worldly absolutisms, secularism is the denial of this human freedom and the imposition of a new bondage. In this respect, secularism is a new phenomenon, for it presupposes the historical process of secularization; it presumes a historical man who has assumed responsibility for his world. Secularism is the claim that some institution or formula of truth is absolute, beyond historicity, beyond the limitation of human perspective. Secularism is secularization become profane or demonic.

Secularism in religion is the substitution of religious structures and authorities for the Gospel. Secularism in the churches is the attempt to preserve a fragment of absolute authority for the churches in a secularized world, denying man's responsibility for his future and making faith secondary to institutional loyalty. If the religious institution can maintain even a partial monopoly on faith and truth, it can preserve its own autonomy against history, fashioning its future and the future of the world on the basis of some unchanging form or truth which it possesses. The churches, in this state of secularism, call men away from historical responsibility to an ahistorical, unchanging truth.

We can see secularism in the struggle between religion and evolution in the past century, for the churches were denying the continuity of man with the temporal process of nature; biologists, on their side, were absolutizing their naturalistic theories. The churches were really betraying the affirmation of the Book of Genesis that man was born of the earth. To be sure, the issue was complicated by a godless thrust in nineteenth century scientific development, growing in part from a struggle by scientists to achieve independence of religious restraints. Moreover, the churches had long treated the myth of creation as a literal account of the process of creation, thus transforming a narrative about man's essential nature into a scientific theory about his temporal existence. Hence, religious leaders felt constrained to defend this theory against the godless forces that were asserting man's continuity with the total evolutionary process of nature. The churches were clinging to a supernatural creation of man against the biblical affirmation of man's creation from the earth.

The Christian theory of a miraculous creation of man, abstracting from the biblical narrative a universal principle, had made man's relationship to nature a confusing problem; his having a body was at the best an embarrassing limitation. Evolutionary theory restored man's relationship to nature but seemed to cast serious doubts upon his eternal destiny. Nevertheless, this secularization of man's scientific knowledge of his past opened the way to an understanding of his destiny in the historical categories of the Bible. Secularized man found himself in nature and history, asking about the ultimate meaning of his existence. He found in the saving history an account of his being chosen and given a future; he found that this contingent, historical life could not be secured against death through any pretensions to a divine substance; he found that the meaning of his life was inseparable from the commitment of that life in responsibility for its future. The struggle over evolution initiated a process of secularization of the Bible which has made possible a recovery of the Bible in its authentic, historical categories. Moreover, the ultimate ground for that secularization is the Protestant doctrine of justification by faith through grace. Man's fellowship with God, man's having a future, is founded on no virtue or quality of his nature but only on God's choice which is His love and promise.

Dogmatism about the Bible or particular "facts" recorded in biblical testimony is a prominent form of secularism in the churches. Secularization implies first, therefore, a break with dogmatism—a recognition of the historicity of religion, its appropriation of the divine self-disclosure in history through faith. Dogmatism, in this sense, is an expression of lack of faith in the God of history. There is nothing absolute about

[45]

the documents or even the record of God's acting, for the testimony to God's self-disclosure is refracted through the finite experience of man. The Bible witnesses to the One who discloses Himself in the brokenness of human history, and it gains its authority only through the One to whom it points, and not through the way in which it points. Sanctification of the way in which the witness is borne, either in the literal statements of the Bible, or in the particular ecclesiastical forms founded upon these events, replaces the presence of the Holy One of Israel with an earthly image. Man is the only earthly image of God, and his history is the only earthly medium of divine disclosure. No book, doctrine or ecclesiastical form can become a substitute for this ever-renewed disclosure of the divine presence in the decisions of history.

Secularism in contemporary Christianity is also expressed as clericalism. This is paradoxical in Protestantism, although it is endemic with Roman Catholicism. The Roman Catholic tradition absolutizes the sacramental process and, by implication, gives an absolute status to the office and activity of the priest. Thus, clericalism or the assertion of the unchangeable character of a sacred office in the church is consistent with the Roman Catholic tradition. However, Protestantism has come to its clericalism in another way. Clericalism is the attempt to project the role of the clergy in the old Christendom into the era of a secular world. Thus, ordained leaders of the churches preempt the responsibility of the laity, treating responsibility in the world as essentially nonreligious, while the activities of the religious institutions are viewed as *the religious works*. This point of view is deeply entrenched in Protestantism today, and, in fact, the term "ministry" is even arrogated to the work of religious professionals in our time. We can see that this is secularism when we realize that the Gospel frees man for his ministry of responsibility in the world and that the work of ministry is the exercise of that responsibility in history. This understanding of man's freedom for history, his freedom to be responsible, raises many questions about the role of the religious professional which must be considered subsequently, but the definition of ministry as the activity of a "religious" functionary is clearly a form of secularism. Clericalism is a modern way of substituting the activity of a religious hierarchy for Christian responsibility in the world.

Secularism also appears in contemporary Christianity in the restriction of the religious life to the private sphere of inner emotional life and intimate relationships. This aspect of secularism has already been examined under the rubric of pietism, but in the present context we can understand that the restriction of the impact of the Gospel to the residential sphere has its basic roots in a denial of the Gospel and a rejection of the sovereignty of God over all of history. Christian preoccupation with the private world of suburbia is not a demographic accident but an explicit apostasy. Residential Christianity is the acme of secularism, the rejection of man's responsibility for mankind in history. The racial segregation, for example, that characterizes this residential Christianity is not simply a historical accident but rather an expression of the rejection of the Gospel in residential Christianity, since the residential sphere deliberately encloses man in a private morality. The historical task in the metropolitan area is the creation of an interdependent metropolis. Pietism is the religious sanction for rejection of that historical responsibility.

Whether secularism appears as absolutizing a religious dogma or preserving a fragment of official authority or segregating a special sphere of life from the rule of faith, in every case the historical task of man as decision for God in history is denied and another authority is substituted for the sovereign Lord of history.

The institutional crisis of the churches is symptomatic of secularism in religious life. The churches will break through this institutional crisis by recognition of the Christian roots of the secularization of the Western world. Not only are the churches called to confirm man in his responsibility for his history, but they are also summoned to face their own need for secularization—for openness to God's rule in history.

Secularism is not confined to the churches, and, indeed, the ministry of the churches is essentially to confirm the world in its responsibility for history. The notion of secularization does not deny the sinfulness of the world in the name of some optimistic view of

[48]

man's possibilities in history. Man is the rebel who claims for himself the role of God. Secularism in the world, against which the Church is called to bear witness, is the arrogation to man of God's sovereignty and the consequent assertion of an absolute claim for man's historical structures. Secularization of the world, which the churches are called upon to affirm, is man's assumption of responsibility for his history in full recognition of the relativity of his perspectives. Secularism, the claim of ultimacy for a conditioned, historical structure, denies man's freedom and substitutes conformity to human authority for responsibility before God.

The dominant form of secularism in the West is the elevation of political or economic structures to absolute status. This is the religious character of the totalitarian movements that have plagued the Western world. They claim to be the structures of history's fulfillment. Underlying all totalitarianism is the affirmation of human autonomy, the claim that man and certain structures of his life are ultimate. The German people fostered this notion in their idolatry of blood and soil. The Russian people have developed an absolute rule of the Communist party by the assertion that they possess the truth of history's final fulfillment. Western nations like the United States have countered these historical absolutes with a tendency to elevate the democratic way of life and the system of private economic enterprise to an absolute status. In each case, certain processes and structures within history are elevated above history, man's responsibility for history is preempted by a particular institution, party or pattern of life. Such idolatrous world views substitute historical structures for God, invoking a deity of some kind as sanction for their claims. The secularism of historical absolutes subjects man's decisions in the present to a human group who claim to possess the future.

This form of secularism, particularly in the absolute state, is so common in the present world that it needs little further comment. The Confessional Church of Germany arose in 1933 with the Barmen Declaration as a "No!" to the absolute state of the Nazi doctrine. The idolatry of Communism and the pretensions of the Democratic way of life present a much more confusing picture; for example, the Amsterdam meeting of the World Council of Churches went no further than indicating its reservations at the absolutizing of either of these interpretations of history. This did not mean that the democratic way of life was simply equated with communistic collectivism. It only warned prophetically that absolutizing the ethos of free enterprise would lead to ultimate destruction for all mankind, even as the ultimate claims of communistic collectivism now threaten to subjugate mankind to the absolute rule of a political party. Invocation of ultimacy for historical structures whether religious, political or economic, is a denial of man's responsibility to search the needs of mankind in their actual historical situations. History is the sphere of free action or it is not history. Responsibility in history is the exercise of this human freedom in answerability to the One in whose image man is made. Sin in history is the substituting of a truth or system in man's possession for the ultimate truth to whom he is answerable.

A more subtle secularism in our day is the domination of life by means; the rule of technique over human good, the transformation of communication into propaganda, the rule of production over the purposes of human life. This is the secularism which infects the metropolitan area; it is a subtle kind of secularism because it arises from the loss of any center for life and culture. Man is freed for historical responsibility through secularization. He is thrown into maturity by the removal of the domination of a religious hierarchy. He faces responsibility to constitute his present world out of a grasp of the future, so that the past is not merely rejected in nihilistic rebellion, but assimilated to the present as a meaningful part of that future. However, society without a center builds its future upon its lust for power and desire for affluence. Freed for history, man turns to his techniques, his inventiveness and skill in order to fabricate a future. The sacred collectivisms attempt to dominate man's future by absolutizing a claim over which the hierarchy maintains control, whereas industrial man surrenders to the future which his technique engenders; hence the groups controlling technical development monopolize power and shape the future. What is available to man in the present is always a means for the realization of a future, but the loss of any grasp upon the future leads to a surrender to the means at hand and to the groups who control those means.

The victory of technique over human values is the fate of secularized man without faith, without a center from which to move confidently toward the future. Here we touch a subtle form of secularism in the contemporary world. Man is cast into history with freedom to grasp the future as a possibility open to him. He is in history with One who confirms his freedom and frees him to live with his fellowman out of the New Mankind—the divine gift. This is life in faith through grace. However, the earthly city rejects this freedom to commit itself to the promise of the New Mankind. Desire replaces faith, possession of the present dominates the future to which man belongs in commitment. The city fashions its own future by substituting productivity, technique, new inventions and better organization for responsibility.

This is the ambiguity of secularization; the productivity of the twentieth century is a consequence of secular man's freedom to explore the universe and dominate nature. This productivity is an expression of human freedom in history. However, the substitution of productivity for responsible decisions about the good of mankind—blind faith in productivity— is a denial of man's responsibility for the use of productivity. The crisis of the affluent societies of the West has arisen as this blind faith in technique and productivity has come into question. Preoccupation with goals in the United States in recent years is symptomatic of this crisis, for men are no longer willing to entrust the future to the blind forces of productivity. They are aware that they cannot forego their responsibility to determine the use of productivity.

The domination of means over ends, of technique over values, can also be seen in the gradual breakdown of communication and the use of words solely to influence and dominate men. The disunity of the city, aggravated by the disappearance of middle levels of political power and the appearance of conflicting factions, lures politicians into an engineering of consent. Political rhetoric becomes the propaganda of bureaucratic organization. Words no longer communicate and create a community of life; they are used to project the interests of a group in power and manipulate those who are powerless. The constant threat of propaganda to dominate all media of communication, whether in advertising or in political maneuvering, reveals the depth of the threat of secularism in the city.

The Task of the Servant Church

Mankind cannot remain free without confidence in the future; men cannot have a history without faith. The proclamation of openness to the future, the call to faith, is the work of the Church in the secularized city. It witnesses to One who will be present for man in the future for which man assumes responsibility;

thus, it grounds man's responsibility for history in a faith which confirms him in his freedom.

The servant Church appears as the expression of God's gracious presence and promise in the midst of secularisms. The emergence of the servant Church is essential to the churches because it struggles against their inclination to absolutize their own structures, freeing them for their task of proclamation in a secularized world. The servant Church is crucial to a secularized world, for it affirms man's freedom for history by declaring the promise that is given to him in history. Amid the disunity and secularism of the city, the Church is the ministering servant of judgment and hope.

Whereas the old Christendom sought to implement a sacred vision by conforming the world to its grasp of truth and using the laity to preserve this sacred truth, the servant Church is the fellowship of those who are conscious of their freedom as men to constitute the future. The laity is not an administrative arm of a hierarchy in the servant Church; the laity *is* the Church in a secularized world. The sphere of religious obedience shifts from the religious organizations to the historical decisions of mankind; hence, where the old Christendom sought to draw men into conformity to the religious organization, fitting all aspects of life to this structure, the servant Church affirms man's freedom for history and strengthens him in the responsible exercise of this freedom. The secularized Church is the laity in its ministry in the world; it is the Church as servant.

We can grasp the distinctive character of the servant Church by distinguishing it from the old Christendom and the Reformation interpretation of the Church in the world. The old Christendom mediated salvation to mankind by arranging all elements of human society and culture in conformity to the sacred truth possessed by the Church, dispensing divine power to each part for the fulfillment of its particular function. The Reformation vision juxtaposed a spiritual kingdom, in which salvation was proclaimed and received in faith, to a worldly kingdom in which men were intended to fear God and conform to the order of institutions or laws which He had ordained for the restraint of sin. The servant Church overcomes the dualistic elements in the Reformation vision by rejecting preordained institutions to which the human kingdom is to be conformed and by affirming man's responsibility to fashion this world in responsibility before God. The Church is no longer an institutional structure of salvation alongside the worldly structures of restraint. The Church is that community within the worldly structures of historical responsibility which recognizes and acknowledges God's gracious work for all mankind. The servant Church is the community who confirm mankind in its freedom to fashion its future, protesting the pretensions to ultimacy in any human structures and suffering with men in the struggle against the powers of evil.

The secularization of the world raises radical questions about the religious organization; by contrast, in the old Christendom, questions arose as to the significance of various tasks *in the world*. Religious duties within the sacramental institution and various special activities such as pilgrimages had a significant relationship to salvation. However, work in the world, whether of a knightly or a servile type, could contribute to salvation only through the special mediations of the sacramental institution. In the perspective of the servant Church, however, the balance is shifted to the ministries within the worldly spheres; the activities within the religious organization become questionable. The historical struggle for the new mankind becomes the arena of man's answerability to God. The ministry of proclamation is still needed in the world, but that task is the work of laity in the various worldly spheres. How religious organizations are or should be related to this historical responsibility, and even what religious activities are necessary to this servanthood, become subjects of debate in the servant Church. The secularization of the world provokes an institutional crisis in the churches because a secularized world finds the locus of salvation in the field of historical responsibility.

When historical responsibility is recognized as the field of Christian life and ministry, the orientation of the churches to the metropolitan struggle is transformed. The churches today see the metropolitan area as a threat to the stability of religious organization. They see racial change as upsetting to the institutional equilibrium of their congregations. They see metropolitan planning as a conspiracy to by-pass their time-honored buildings and partition their hardwon areas of affluence. This is not said in a cynical spirit, for most of the organizations of the metropolitan area look at urban development in this way. They are concerned to exploit the urban environment on behalf of their organizational interests; every change threatens to upset their previous calculations of advantage. Once the servanthood of the Church becomes the lens through which metropolitan struggles are perceived, the churches begin to ask about possibilities of ministry and the role of change in realizing human interdependence. This is no utopian vision but only a different conception of the nature and task of the Church. If the churches were called to increase their religious activities in the midst of rapid metropolitan change, they would have to become factions lobbying for changes that were suitable to their organizational interests. If their task is servanthood in the emerging metropolis, their ministry is to participate in public life on behalf of a human environment in the metropolis.

The churches, despite the institutional crisis, believe that they only have to do business as usual. This illusion is perpetuated principally by the insulated character of their residential base. They search frantically for techniques to improve their activities, and yet each renewal movement leads to further isolation from the metropolitan struggle. However, the servant Church takes the secularized world seriously; it acknowledges the limited role of residential congregations. The values of the residential community—personal equilibrium, emotional adjustment and the care of children in family life—form important aspects of humanity. This is the matrix from which personality emerges in health or disorder; consequently, the ministry of the servant Church cannot turn away from residential communities in disdain or neglect. Nevertheless, this residential context of life cannot provide a platform for servanthood in the struggle for metropolis. This residential community is insulated against that struggle by its private, consumer character in a technological society. To be sure, residential life needs to be intimately related to the public struggle for its own well-being; metropolis will realize its fulfillment only when residential life also expresses interdependence and social responsibility. The truly private values also need to be recovered from the externality of residential association. However, the public spheres of social, economic, educational and political life will have to provide the main fields of ministry for the servant Church in coming decades; moreover, ministries in these public spheres need to be closely linked to Christian communities in the residential context, so that residential life may be accorded its appropriate place as a private structure in the formation of metropolis.

The consideration of clericalism has already made clear that ministry takes on a different significance in the servant Church. In the churches today, ministry is usually taken to mean what a clergyman does in and for the religious organization. In the servant Church, ministry is servanthood within the world. Ministry is discerning the promise of the saving history in the historical decisions of public responsibility; ministry is also discerning the truly human in the spheres of personal association and family life. In a secularized world, ministry is realized in the decisions for a responsible society. Thus, the position of the theological specialist is auxiliary to the ministry. Those who are especially ordained for sacramental celebration also have ministries in the servant Church, but their ministry is to equip the Church in its witness and servanthood in the world. This shift in the character of ministry can be dramatized thus: the ministry is usually conceived today as the work of clergymen with auxiliary aids among the laity; ministry in the servant Church is the work of laity in the world with auxiliary help from theological specialists.

Secularization issues from the appropriation of the Gospel, for as men receive deliverance from bondage to the powers of this world they can assume responsibility for their history in this world. The notion of progress which played such a crucial role in the late nineteenth century glimpsed this truth but refracted it through the lens of scientistic thought. The secularization of the world is progress toward human freedom and responsibility; however, this progress signifies increasing freedom to shape the future as creative or destructive and not the automatic realization of the good society through scientific understanding. Secularization is always potentially secularism. Hence, the notion of secularization contradicts both the theological liberalism which gives unqualified affirmation to natural processes and the neo-orthodoxy which despairs of human initiative and responsibility. Secularization recognizes history and its problems of meaning as the sphere of man's struggle for salvation. In history, man is freed to constitute his world. In this respect, a secularized world recognizes the biblical world of divine action in history as congruent with its own existence in history. The renewal of biblical theology becomes a vital necessity rather than a legalistic requirement in a secularized world, for man discovers the meaning of his own history in reflection on biblical history, even as he appropriates the biblical disclosure only in reflection on his own historical decisions. Secularization has not led man away from the Christian message; rather, the dogmatisms and literalisms which close the Bible to contemporary man are transcended in this new world, and men see themselves confronting their salvation in historical decision. The categories of biblical faith are freed from their miraculous and supernaturalistic garments, becoming consonant with the categories of historical responsibility in which men live. The pretensions of economic forces and social collectivities are recognized, moreover, as signs of idolatry in history, for the One through whom men are freed for history confirms them in their freedom against their own pretensions to finality. Thus, secularization makes a legitimate claim upon the churches to assume the form of the servant—the form of their Lord in the world, making no pretense to take His place but only seeking to be conformed to Him in that place where they are called.

If the sphere of history is the arena of man's salvation, then what role, if any, can be ascribed to religious organizations? We have tended to equate loyalty to Christ with loyalty to the institutional churches. What possible meaning can one give to loyalty to the Christian fellowship and its institutional obligations, when Christian faith is response to the presence and claims of Christ in the historical struggle for the New Mankind? These are some of the difficult questions which confront the servant Church in a secularized world. One begins to ask what, if anything, the Church has to do with the case. Why are men not simply called to be human in their historical obligations, for this is man's true end and his salvation?

Instead of losing its validity, the Church fulfills its true task of proclamation through its servanthood in a secularized world. This is its distinctive mission in a world which no longer cringes before supernaturalistic powers. We can dramatize this new situation if we recall Premier Khrushchev's remarks when the first Soviet astronaut made his flight. Khrushchev pointed out that the astronaut had demonstrated that no god inhabited the skies. Soviet science had defied the illusory deity. A thoughtful clergyman pointed out, at this time, that it was not so easy to dismiss Khrushchev's point, even though his theology was somewhat crude. He noted that many Christians had this kind of god who inhabited the skies and could be ejected by some feat of science. However such a god is conceived, he is not the God of the biblical testimony as we understand it today, and he is certainly not a credible deity to contemporary man. This is a world in which astronauts do eject man's petty supernaturalisms from the sky. This is a world which struggles for meaning in and through history and not by escape from history or by flight beyond history. This is the secularized world in which proclamation is discerning the meaning of the human enterprise, in which mission is commitment to that meaning in decisions and actions. It is precisely because the astronaut discredits the petty supernaturalisms and poses the question of the ultimate meaning of man's creative powers that the secularized world needs the testimony of the Church. However, this testimony ceases to be the testimony of the Church when it attempts to subjugate man's reason by asserting sacred facts or waving inviolable texts or canonizing irrefutable dogmas. The rapid expansion of education in a technological world not only discredits such supernaturalism but paves the way for authentic proclamation.

The task of proclamation in the servant Church, the work of the laity as apostolate and ministry, presents a special difficulty in this secularized world. Only as the churches appreciate this problem can they grasp the scope of the work that lies ahead. When the churches maintained their apostolate to the world by enlisting loyalty to religious activities and institutions, the burden of Christian reflection and teaching could be carried by religious specialists. The center of gravity for the continuity of the Gospel in the world was to be found in the highly institutionalized activities of the religious establishment. The most elaborate expression of this machinery in Christianity was the development of the sacramental system of medieval Catholicism by the Fourth Lateran Council in 1215. However, the Lutheran, Anglican and Presbyterian traditions as well as many others have had their own systems of indoctrination and conformity. In each case, the burden of continuity is borne by religious specialists and the laity become passive spectators.

The secularization of the world terminates this traditional structure of continuity, for it rests the heavy burden of apostolate on the laity in their work in the world. The servant Church emerges as a community of highly sensitive and theologically self-conscious laymen. The religious specialists can no longer bear the burden of Christian reflection and teaching; they can only share in this apostolate through their work with laity. The institutional crisis of Christianity has already provoked a consciousness of lay responsibility, as can be seen from innumerable developments of lay theological study. However, most of these movements in the United States have been directed toward strengthening organizational loyalty to religious activities. Their value is repeatedly measured by increases in church statistics. To this extent, the churches have failed to see the significance of this emerging lay consciousness.

We confront a paradox in the religious situation, for religious preoccupation gives way to responsibility in history in a secularized world, and yet the laity then have to assume quite a new burden of theological reflection and sensitivity. The laity can no longer relegate the apostolate to religious specialists. They bear the burden of discerning the meaning of events in the human struggle. The crucial role of the Church in a secularized world only becomes clear as it is seen in the servanthood of the laity in that world. Our task now is to consider what such an apostolate involves in a secularized world.

CHAPTER III

The Prophetic Fellowship

We live in an organizational society; this is a society which is directed and shaped by the purposeful organization of activities in massive structures. The Church *in* such a world is the Church engaged with these directing forces of the world; moreover, that engagement is possible only through a sensitive and committed laity. Any embodiment of the Church in contemporary society will be an apostolate of the laity in the world. This is the crucial fact about renewal of the Church in an organizational world.

For some decades there has been discussion of the role of the laity; indeed, excellent books have been devoted entirely to consideration of the lay movement in the churches. The crucial question remains, however, as to precisely how an apostolate of the laity can carry the proclamation of the Church. Whenever the issue of lay ministry arises in the churches, religious leaders and organizations claim to be working toward a witnessing laity. These views of the laity assume that the religious organizations can be the fountainhead for development of this apostolate of the laity: the various spheres of the world are the field of witness for the laity; the church gathers in an assembly to hear preaching and to share a sacramental fellowship; the church then disperses for its apostolate in the world. The religious organization is conceived as the nurturing center of the witnessing laity. The world is the field of witness or apostolate for this laity. The only difficulty is that actually there is no such apostolate. There is a chasm between gathering and dispersing.

Such a view of the apostolate misconceives the nature of contemporary society and the depth of the alienation of the churches from the dynamic forces of our world. The training of an apostolate has to occur where the laity find themselves engaged *in* worldly responsibilities. The platform for mission is the organizational structure shaping this world. Once the Church accepts her calling to be a living testimony of the Spirit in the world, she has to forego a safe anchorage in the cultic body or confessional assembly. The medieval and Reformation forms of the Church embodied the Message in the familial web of society.

[66]

Once this web is broken and replaced by organizational forces, as it is in contemporary society, a new form of the Church is needed.

Religious leaders have been unable or unwilling to face the alienation of the churches from the dynamic of the contemporary world; hence, they deny the inadequacy of the inherited structure of the churches. Repeated attempts to organize a lay apostolate have demonstrated the inadequacy of religious structures; but these religious leaders continue to pour forth a rhetoric of renewal; thus the lay apostolate degenerates into one more organizational program of the religious enterprise.

The religious institutions face a choice in the contemporary world: (1) they can strengthen their confessional assemblies in the residential enclaves and provide a religious refuge, leaving the world to seek its own peace; or (2) they can relinquish the comforts of these enclaves and become involved with the organizational structures that shape our emerging society. The former possibility, the organization church, is most attractive to religious professionals because it guarantees affluence to the churches, albeit at the cost of more ulcers and nervous breakdowns for the religious leaders, not to mention an impoverished proclamation. The second possibility, secularization of the churches, poses serious threats to institutional stability but opens the way to direct engagement with the principalities and powers that dominate our lives. The organization church is the affluent church; it is the

Church of the middle class. The secularized Church is mission in an organizational society; it is the servant Church in history. Many religious leaders would like to combine these approaches, but they soon discover that the residential enclaves swallow up the religious enterprise in private interests.

Apostolate as Historical Reflection

The lay apostolate will require new forms of worship and gathering, but these forms can only be determined by the task of proclamation. Hence, the principal question is the nature of proclamation in an organizational society. The contemporary stalemate in the development of the lay apostolate has arisen largely from the attempt to work within the older forms of the Church. Once we become clear on the process of proclamation in a complex society, we can move toward forms appropriate to the apostolate. The work of proclamation is decisive to the embodiment of the Church, and it is this work which is so much in question in our secularized world.

Proclamation takes the form of *theological reflection* in a secularized world. *Reflection* is a coming to consciousness in the consideration of the present meaning of events. This is the radical reorientation confronting the Church in the contemporary world. This perspective alters the character of the apostolate and the role of the religious professional, but it also changes the context in which the churches fulfill their calling.

[68]

There are, of course, many other meanings of the term "reflection"; in the work of apostolate, however, reflection is the opening of experience to its depth dimensions—to its questions of meaning in a proximate and ultimate sense. In reflection, we halt the stream of reality which flows into the present and sweeps us ahead; we consider who we are in the light of present expectations, future projects and ultimate commitments. Thus, the determinations of the past are transcended and reconstituted; we decide our future and reshape our past. I am not simply a product of my past. I adopt and re-create this past as my own project. Reflection is the mode of thought that takes seriously man's historicity—his living out of a past on behalf of a future. Reflection is the mode of being of historical and secular man. Reflection, at least as interpreted here, denies that the human mind can apprehend a fixed reality transcending experience which provides an unchanging criterion for faith and action. Man's reason is not divine; it is even as man, a historical event. The reflective process assumes the creaturely character of man's reason and decisions, which is to say that man not only has a history but is his history. Man constitutes himself, thus, in his decisions for the future; faith, as decision for the future, is the essence of his being in the world as a meaningful enterprise.

Christian reflection starts from the historicity of man; it asks about his identity in the light of the saving events in which the meaning of his enterprise is disclosed. However, the identity disclosed in the saving history is no objective identity; Christian reflection acknowledges that even the identity disclosed in the saving events is only man's identity as he appropriates it in projecting his own future; reflective participation in the saving history is the opening of one's own history to ultimate questioning and hope. Faith in Jesus as the Christ is acknowledgment that Jesus discloses who I am; to be in Christ, thus, is to come to myself, to recognize myself, to come to my true identity. I discover the meaning of my past through Him. I become conscious of my true being. Christian reflection is testing in decision for my future the congruity between my own history and the decisive event of human history—Jesus as the Christ. Hence, engagement in the world, responsibility for shaping that world, becomes the milieu of proclamation, and ultimately the proper milieu of confession and worship.

Discerning the meaning of events is the stuff of daily life. Reflection is no esoteric activity of hooded monks; it is the common activity of all men who question their motives and the meanings of the actions which others take toward them. That men often refuse to reflect is only symptomatic of their anxiety and fear. Christian reflection deepens this personal process of consideration by opening both past and future to questioning in the light of God's saving actions for man. We normally hide our past, even from ourselves. It is painful to dredge up those broken relationships, hurts and unhealed feelings of guilt; indeed, this inability to have our past as part of our present is what we mean by guilt. The broken relationships of the past continue to dominate our present moments, since we must do everything in our power to conceal from ourselves and others the true extent of our inadequacy and unworthiness. To have one's past, to be able to accept and appropriate that past as a meaningful part of the present, to allow that past to be really past and not the unconscious ruler of the present: this is what it means to be forgiven, to be justified. The saving history restores this past to its true place by declaring even its distortions as occasions of the life-giving and life-sustaining presence of God; even our suppression of those feelings of guilt had made possible some kind of life in this world. This recovery of the past in Christian reflection issues, however, from the discovery that we have a future; it is only in the light of this promise of a future, this assurance of our identity as children of God and fellow heirs with Christ, that we can own this broken past for what it is. The work of Christian reflection, thus, is the discovery of our true history, our true identity, through that history in which God has chosen us—the history of His life for us in Jesus as the Christ.

The work of the servant Church is to engage the world in reflection on the meaning of its history, to summon men to the search for the meaning of the events in which they are engaged. This is *the aposto-*

late of the servant Church; it reflects with the world on the present meaning of the saving history. This form of apostolate is essentially the prophetic ministry of proclamation; the apostolate of the laity is the discerning of God's history as mediated in the events of our history before God, and this is precisely *the task of prophecy.* The call to reflection is a call to judgment and promise in a world which has surrendered itself to technique, propaganda and threats of massive retaliation.

The servant Church is not simply serving men on their terms; it serves God by ministering in judgment and promise within the structures of man's world. The laity is, thus, the prophetic fellowship which summons men to reflection upon their responsibility for shaping the future. This prophetic fellowship has no special program or political party; it has only the commitment to the New Mankind which God has created in his Son, the mankind of love and reconciliation which discloses the true being of all men and their life together. In the name of this future to which all men belong and which is theirs to acknowledge, the prophetic fellowship summons men and women in every walk of life to consider this gift as disclosing their true identity and ultimate hope.

The apostolate of the servant Church takes the form, therefore, of the *prophetic fellowship,* discerning God's promise and presence in the midst of the creativity as well as opaqueness of man's historical responsibility. This prophetic fellowship of laity cannot find a comfortable place within the religious establishments any more than the Old Testament prophets; the sphere of man's historical responsibility is the only milieu in which this apostolate can be exercised. The prophetic fellowship, unlike previous forms of apostolate in the Christian Church, takes man's responsibility to shape the future with utmost seriousness. Two other forms of apostolate in Christian history have stressed other moments in the saving history: the medieval or cultic Church participated in the world as a restored, supernatural creation to which all parts of life were to be accorded; the Reformation Church or confessional assembly set itself in juxtaposition to the world as a gathering of elect or believers whose presence leavened the world and even transformed elements within the world but never identified itself fully in Christ with the destiny of that world. The servant Church in a secularized world, the prophetic fellowship, stands within the milieu of the historical responsibility of mankind, acknowledging with men and before God their true identity as the New Mankind, the New Creation, in the shaping of this world. Even as our world has moved into an entirely new historical era, the form of apostolate is slowly assuming a radically new form.

Proclamation as reflection contrasts sharply with the cultic and confessional forms of proclamation. The Church as cultic body saves man from the world of existence by incorporating him into a mystical organism. The cultic Church proclaims the Good News through actions or rituals by which the whole of life is conformed with its suprahistorical goal. Men, women and children are incorporated into this mystical life which intersects vertically with the world as a miraculous, spiritual body. This mystical organism maintains channels of communication with the world through liturgical rites and the continuing fidelity of its members. Proclamation, then, is the re-presentation of Christ in cultic acts, whether in the initiatory rite of baptism, in the revitalizing event of eucharist or in the matrimonial process. Proclamation is the *cultic* life itself, and faith is conformity to cultic truth. The Church is, thus, that miraculous organism which mediates eternal life to the members. Salvation and cultic participation become inseparable.

The power of such a cultic mode of proclamation inheres in its universal enduring form in the world. The cultic church lives out of a sacred past, representing that past in a continual re-creation of those saving events, and thus releasing men from fear of the future. The cultic body shields man against historical responsibility. In the categories of historical reflection, the cultic mode of proclamation replaces man's history with membership in a trans-historical body; until the final day, of course, society continues, but man's true society is the Church; the end of history is a Church. The task of proclamation, therefore, is one of incorporating "souls" into this mystical organism, this superhumanity, and disciplining human society so that a minimal order can be preserved until the cultic body is all in all.

Many attempts have been made to modify the cultic mode of proclamation, particularly among Anglicans, and, indeed, the cultic body often resembles a confessional assembly in post-Reformation traditions. However, the pure type of cultic proclamation presumes an unchanging and universal form through which mankind may participate in its true end. The Church is present only when this universal form is present. The cultic body overcomes anxiety about the future by denying change; the future is already in possession, since it is immured within this cultic form.

By contrast, *the confessional assembly* proclaims a present relationship of forgiveness, wrought in the past but effective now and to eternity. This salvation is announced through cult and preaching, but the relationship does not depend upon these acts. The focus of the confessional assembly is, thus, upon the present moment as receiving and acknowledging in gratitude what has already been done once for all in the past— the life with God brought about in the saving history. These events are not really past history, since they are present with power in the proclamation within the assembly. The Church *becomes* in hearing this message.

There are, of course, many variations of this mode of proclamation; after the breakdown of the cultic body in the West, various styles of confessional assembly have arisen. Nevertheless, the emphasis in the confessional assembly is upon the present acceptance of a relationship to God established in the saving history; the principal moment is the meaning of the present in the light of the past. Hence, the crucial work of proclamation is preaching, for the principal issue is to acknowledge this relationship which God has initiated. In fact, in the confessional assembly proclamation usually means preaching, since the established relationship becomes present reality through the work of the Spirit in confirming this Good News *in* the hearer. Proclamation takes on definitive meaning by emphasizing the present relationship to the fact in contrast to the cultic stress on membership in a mystical body which perpetuates the past into the future. Thus, baptism becomes a sign of inward acceptance of this relationship of forgiveness, which gives rise to the pressure within confessional traditions toward adult baptism in which the relationship can be explicitly acknowledged and even experienced. The Lord's Supper becomes both reminder of the work through which the relationship of justification was effected and a sign of the present reality of that justification. The universal scope of the expression *Word of God* in the confessional assembly reveals this stress on the mediation of the saving relationship through announcement of the message.

At the risk of exaggerating the difference between cultic and confessional proclamation, one can say that the cultic body assures man of a future by incorporat-

ing him into a mystical body already in possession of
that future; by contrast, the confessional assembly
brings the full power of the saving event into the
present moment through preaching, rooting a man in
a trustworthy past which no fearful future can shake.
In both forms of proclamation the future is safe-
guarded through the holy past: in the cultic body,
the holy past is a universal form moving changelessly
through history; in the confessional assembly the past,
the saving event, is the real history and man's calling
is to refer himself back to this real history, so that he
will be free from fear in the present and the future.
Both forms of proclamation shift attention away from
the future toward the past: the cultic body turns attention toward obedience to an institution which mediates this past; the confessional assembly focuses men
on a relationship already established in the past, calling for acknowledgment and gratitude.

Historical man knows himself to be responsible for
the constitution of his future; he also has to cope
with the past and the saving history, but his basic orientation is toward the future which he is called to
create; he can affirm the eternal presence of the past
in cultic forms of reenactment, but he cannot consign
his responsibility for history to a cultic organization
without denying the world to which God has called
him. He can acknowledge the decisive character of
the saving event which is so central to the confessional
assembly, finding trust in this covenant community,
but not as a history which is discontinuous with his

[77]

own history as decision for the future. We can consider these *three modes* of proclamation in terms of the three moments of man's history with God: cultic proclamation incorporates man into a restored creation; confessional proclamation lifts him to a present state of redemption; prophetic proclamation opens him to a future which he is empowered to create. Each is a kind of history, to be sure, but only the prophetic proclamation finds man's present responsibility as the crucial medium of God's presence.

A dualism between Church and world issues from the focus upon the transcendent faith relationship in the confessional assembly. Only the believers or the elect stand within the true relationship of justification, and yet the believers have wordly obligations among the nonbelievers; thus, the Church's transformation of the world is conceived as a leavening of a wicked world through the presence of the believers. These believers may seek to correct and purify the legal and social practices of the world; even this activity in the world, however, is conceived as announcing the Good News, since acknowledgment of one's justification by Christ's work is expressed through confession in the assembly and purity of life in the world. Despite the importance of purity in the world, however, man's true history is his relationship with God through Christ—a transcendent history. The mundane history is to be tolerated or even made exemplary, but it is always a lesser history, if not actually irrelevant.

The Church as prophetic fellowship has a different

[78]

understanding of proclamation. This mode of proclamation, as we have already noted, arises in the context of a secularized world. Prophetic proclamation through summons to reflection is an opening of everyday experience in the light of the saving history; it sees man's present history as his true history and the future which he shapes as his real future. To call the biblical events holy is to affirm that they are the paradigmatic events in which the ultimate meanings of our contemporary experience are disclosed. The saving history is holy, however, because it discloses the depth of our own history; our history authenticates this history as saving history. The meaning of present experience is the crucial question for prophetic proclamation, but this present experience is perceived in terms of its ultimate possibilities.

Historical reflection is, of course, concerned with the *interrelations* of past, present and future rather than with isolating one moment of the temporal sequence. Nevertheless, historical reflection takes its point of departure from the relation of the *future to the present;* by contrast, the cultic proclamation is concerned with the relations between the sacred past and the future, and the confessional assembly is preoccupied with the relation of the sacred past to the present. In contrast to the cultic body, prophetic proclamation discovers true identity within present events rather than by squeezing experience into a cultic form which is above history. The cultic body creates my true being through ritual acts, thus incorporating me

[79]

into the sacred substance. Prophetic proclamation discloses my true being in the New Mankind in which I now participate and which I am called to create.

The obvious question is what, then, does the saving history bring into my present experience? The Gospel is deliverance from the guilt and anxiety which blot out the future. Sin is denial of one's historicity, the assumption that one is oneself origin rather than co-creator of the future. Sin is, thus, essentially a denial that one is one's history, an event which cannot contain its own meaning but moves toward meaning. The saving history is the promise of meaning even to those who deny their search for meaning.

Let us return at this point to our earlier reference to guilt, our understanding of man's inability to accept the past as his own past—our guilt is the sign that we cannot accept this past as our own; our past is alienated from us. There is no deliverance from such guilt except forgiveness, since man is the one who in pride and lust denied to others their true identity and rejected their membership in the New Mankind. Such forgiveness is mediated, through the human community, but it is disclosed as the foundation of humanity in the events of the saving history. Man's life and history are renewed day by day in forgiving love; they are opened to the future through this acceptance. Until man can have his past and see it for his own, he cannot have an authentic identity and history; without forgiveness he must shape all of his acts in the present in order to conceal his past from himself

and from others, and he must anticipate the future
not as possibility but as a threat that he will be dis-
covered for who he really is. Life becomes a conspiracy of deceit rather than a work of disclosure. To
be baptized and to appropriate this baptism inwardly
in reflection is to recognize that forgiveness is more
than an accidental encounter in an otherwise destructive life, for the saving event discloses forgiveness as
the foundation of the New Mankind; to be baptized
is to begin one's history, for one has received one's
past as a gift in which God was present preserving and
saving life. Even the guilt which seemed so destructive
is disclosed as a saving link with one's true history, for
it prevented an utter resignation to nonauthentic existence. The guilt is disclosed as a divine discontent
and forgiveness is seen as man's true mode of being
in the world. In this moment, the prophetic fellowship is at one with the emphasis of the confessional
assembly.

The Gospel also delivers man from the anxiety
which closes out the future. Even as guilt fills the
present with the fear of being disclosed for who one
really is, so anxiety over the responses of others and
over the course of events leads to the attempt to control the future. Bondage to the Law, the struggle to
preserve a *status quo*, the unwillingness to listen to
others and hear their authentic claims, the narrowing
of one's opening upon the world so that new events
are not really experienced; these and many other forms
of closure issue from anxiety about the future. Where

guilt diminishes openness in the present world, anxiety reduces openness to the future. Man's history is either impoverished or utterly foreclosed in this bondage to Law or ritualized experiences. However, his link with authentic existence is maintained by that very fear and anxiety which now enslave him to petty legalisms and rituals. Deliverance from this bondage is mediated through the human community, but it finds its source in the promise of being present in the anxiety-ridden future, even when that future means annihilation as in the Cross. Where he fears absence, betrayal and loss, he is reassured by the promise of continuing presence. This promise of continuing presence is rooted in the saving history; God gives us His Word to be with us in any and all futures. The Gospel is a resurrection faith for it is promise of continuing presence in the midst of alienation.

The Eucharistic celebration is the reenactment of the saving event in this prophetic fellowship; its crucial note is promise of continuing presence—the eschatological proclamation that man belongs to the future. In the Eucharist, the community professes its true life as showing forth in its fellowship the living presence of its Lord. The account of the Eucharist in I Corinthians 11 makes it quite evident that St. Paul conceived the Eucharistic event as primarily an embodiment of this New Mankind within the community, showing forth the risen Body and discerning this Body as the New Mankind.

Thus, proclamation as summons to reflection does

not relegate the Gospel to a merely exemplary history or to the declaration of a romantic ideal. The prophetic community begins in the forgiveness that issues from the saving history and is mediated through its own community. To have a history, to be responsible for the future, is to be received as one truly is with one's past. Moreover, this community can be reflective, can open itself to the present, and struggle to fashion a future which takes full account of the present situation, because this community is founded in a promise of presence and mediates this promise through its own life. We could call this prophetic fellowship a community of faithfulness, for its being *in* the world and its openness to the future *of* the world form its essential apostolate. We had a parable of this community of reflection in the flurry over private bomb shelters in the early sixties. The Christian community cannot authentically undertake anything but a communal program of shelters, for it cannot break its commitment to be a sign of continuing presence with the world in whatever future this world may encounter. Acceptance of the past (the confessional witness) and availability in the present (the cultic witness) open mankind to the future, but acceptance and availability are in turn a consequence of receiving the promise of a future (the prophetic testimony). Jeremiah purchasing a piece of land in the ravaged country—a sign of continuing presence—is the parable of the prophetic fellowship.

The Church as prophetic fellowship has close af-

finity with the Church as confessional assembly; however, it separates from the main stream of this tradition in rejecting the dual history and dual loyalty of
the confessional assembly. The secularized world has
only the history in which it is engaged; any authentic
meaning is encountered there, any ultimate fulfillments are present there, at least in foretaste. The
Church as prophetic fellowship has no escape hatches
from this history into a superhistory; she is only open
to the same history and more committed to shape the
same future for which she knows herself responsible.
To be sure, the tradition of the confessional assembly
is very diverse and some strands approximate the prophetic fellowship more than others. The prophetic
fellowship is not inheritor of an accomplished history
of salvation but partner with Christ in the constitution of the New Mankind in history. This work is
possible through the divine initiative in Jesus as the
Christ; it is empowered now through divine presence
in the decisions for the future; but it is man's work
because this is the future which he is called to create.
The essential mode of being in the confessional assembly is trust; the crucial moment of the prophetic
fellowship is commitment.

The people of metropolis know themselves to be
responsible for the shape of the emerging society, but
they hesitate before this responsibility. The Church
confirms metropolis in its openness to the future. In
saying this, we have to discriminate clearly between
the Church as prophetic fellowship and the churches

of the metropolitan areas. The Church exists in the churches but she also exists in unacknowledged form among men and women who are committed to metropolis but not to religious organization. The apostolate of the laity in metropolis is to deepen reflection upon the present situation in the light of the future which we are given in Christ. The authentic Church only emerges in this process of reflection and decision-making. The task of proclamation, then, is one of evoking the Church, awakening authentic Christianity to consciousness in the midst of the metropolitan struggle.

To say this is not simply to write off the churches and their organizational preoccupation. The churches reveal endless variety in their concerns and religious styles. Prejudgments on these matters are not the work of apostolate. The summons to reflection is extended to churches and other structures of the society; men and women are called to consider the future for which they are responsible in the light of the saving history in which they are promised a future as the New Mankind.

The Church as prophetic fellowship is actually functioning now in our society. The servant Church is not, in other words, simply an ecclesiastical utopia. The reflective understanding of apostolate has already won the day in the field of personal, pastoral care; a new grasp of the meaning of baptism and of membership in the Church is already issuing from this work in pastoral care. A similar process has occurred in the field of group life, where the interpersonal world as mediation of redemption has opened a whole new perspective on the educational process. A third major development of the reflective apostolate is evident in the emergence of the lay academies as centers of dialogue for men and women engaged in the shaping of our world. The academy movement, whatever its present limitations, represents a foretaste of the prophetic fellowship in metropolis, for it engages men in a reflective process which is deeply implicated in their vocational commitments. This is the work of apostolate in a secularized world. Hence, as we turn to the specific implications of this understanding of proclamation for the metropolitan struggle, we are not considering an abstract possibility but projecting ourselves into the arena of the renewal movements that are stirring the Church in our time.

Engagement in the Metropolitan Struggle

The major obstacle to historical responsibility in urban life is fear. A desperate fear clutches at urban people today—fear of social difference, fear of depression, fear of catastrophic war, fear of neighbors encroaching upon one's bomb shelter. Here we encounter the truth of the oversimplified charge that ours is a materialistic world, since this fear is generated primarily by desire to maintain the world which we have. This desire to possess gives way to fear, because desire increases man's dependence upon what he has or may gain. Fear of loss blots out the awareness of our common interdependence in metropolis; it leads to shortsighted attempts to erect walls of segregation; it hardens stereotypes by which we legitimize our closure to other people. The vicious circle of desire, fear and despair monopolizes the minds of metropolitan people; thus responsibility for shaping metropolis gives way before the rush to protect local interests; men become so obsessed with fear that they blot out or impoverish the future which they sought to protect.

The prophetic fellowship is the community which is aware of the New Mankind to which we belong in Christ; it is the authentic Church open to the real future and living in the actual present. The character of that future is being created in the historical struggle of mankind, though its figure is only dimly perceived and much of its content is hidden from our sight. The prophetic fellowship is not foisting a trans-historical world upon metropolitan society; it is summoning men and women to openness toward their real future. The laity, in the diverse places where they exercise their responsibilities, are encouraging consideration of the authentic mankind to which men belong and against which they are rebelling. The continuing presence and faithfulness of this prophetic fellowship in the midst of fear marks it as apostolate in the world; indeed, this community has some notion, albeit incomplete and relative, of the character of metropolis, and this awareness provokes the deepest fears within the society. Prophecy carries with it the suffering of servanthood.

The prophetic fellowship engages the world in dialogue on a somewhat different level of reflection from its own ultimate commitment. The apostolate discusses man and not God. Even in their profoundest fears, men reveal the humanity for which they yearn. The struggle for humanity is the common ground of this dialogue. This is the point of encounter for deepening consideration of responsibility. The prophetic fellowship universalizes the values which men cherish for themselves; thus, the segregationist who cherishes privacy and individual choice in association discovers that he cannot enjoy this choice in the final analysis unless it is shared by all mankind. The prophetic fellowship witnesses in the world by disclosing to the world its real future—pointing the way to life in the midst of death. Men who attack the humanity of others do so only on the assumption that there is a humanity (presumably their own) by which they judge; the prophetic fellowship, like Nathan with David after the slaying of Uriah the Hittite, recalls the world to the humanity against which it rebels. The task of proclamation is to hold before society the things which belong to its peace, while affirming those things which society acknowledges to be its true peace. To engage in such an apostolate means freedom from the fear of loss, participation in the New Mankind to which we belong, and risk of the position that we now possess. The servant Church in the churches and latent in the society is that community which manifests this freedom as sacrifice.

Although we cannot give extended consideration to the image of the good society that underlies metropolis, it may be suggestive to consider the general nature of this point of contact for historical reflection. Metropolitan people cherish opportunities; they hope to benefit from the variety of urban culture while still avoiding the destructive conflicts that spread everywhere in this rapidly changing environment. However, the desire for cultural enrichment inescapably brings a responsibility to deal creatively with social change. This double-mindedness, hope for enrichment and fear of change, has led urban people to exploit the cultural richness of urban life while building walls against social and racial change. They wish to aggrandize themselves through the cultural interdependence of metropolis while protecting themselves against the personal interdependence upon which these opportunities ultimately depend.

The prophetic fellowship participates in this metropolitan history and therefore knows its fears. The servant Church is not a Church insulated against these claims and counterclaims, pretending to a false neutrality in the struggle. The lay apostolate know that the New Mankind to which all men belong actualizes human interdependence; indeed, they know that cultural enrichment and personal fulfillment are possible only through personal interdependence. To exclude men from the people to whom they belong is ultimately to deprive them and ourselves of the humanity to which all of us are called. Having and belonging are inseparable for man; the Supreme Court of the United States of America recognized this in 1954 in the decision that separate is not equal. The prophetic fellowship knows that impoverishment through separateness affects those who build the wall even more than those whom they exclude. The vicious circle of urban renewal and blight will not be broken until the human interdependence of metropolis is acknowledged in concrete programs for equality of opportunity in residence, education, employment and human fraternity. Metropolis will not be culturally and spiritually enriching until it acknowledges the human interdependence upon which it is founded; indeed, the metropolitan world will become a wasteland without participation in the New Mankind. The acknowledgment of human interdependence involves first and foremost the giving of respect to those with whom our lives are interwoven in the New Mankind; that respect, moreover, finds its acknowledgment in legal safeguards, personal testimony and concrete fulfillments. Apostolate is witness to the New Mankind amid the old mankind, testimony to the openness of life amid the closure of death.

The creation of metropolis is obstructed by fear, anxiety and guilt. The prophetic fellowship is not concerned to win man's attention away from this struggle to a religious concern. To be sure, the servant Church faces serious difficulties in giving form to its life and we shall be considering the "religious" problems of the prophetic fellowship subsequently; but its essential task is to bring men to consciousness of their history, to recognition of the decisions that they face and to the freedom that is theirs in openness toward the future. This task brings into focus the paradox of secularized Christianity: its demand that the laity, who represent the secular, become theologically far more astute than at any other period in Christian history. Secular Christianity is truly theological in its life. Men and women today are qualified for this task. The Church as cultic body fulfilled the theological task for mankind through the rituals and symbols of the mystical society into which men were incorporated. The Church as cultic body was eminently fitted in this respect for a society which lacked cognitive skills and verbal abilities, and yet its cultic preoccupation also limited the cognitive development of that society. The Church as confessional assembly consigns the theological task to a trained élite who preoccupy themselves with theological questions on behalf of the congregations. Training of the clergy, and general study of the Bible are the principal modes of handling theological work in the confessional assembly. Since the confessional assembly constantly refers itself to a sacred event in the past, study of the saving history is really intended for all and literacy is stimulated. Nevertheless, specialists dominate this theological work and the laity become passive. The prophetic fellowship, engaged as it is in the historical struggles of the world, places the burden of theological work upon its laity in the world. This is the essential nature of the servant Church, for it is a theologically conscious community which is committed to historical responsibility in the world. This does not mean that only theological experts can participate in this prophetic fellowship, for theological reflection is not simply a matter of abstract processes of thought. Some of the deepest theological perception in Christian history has come from laity who penetrated to the roots of existence in the light of the work of Christ. One thinks, for example, of the witness of the disciples, the simple wisdom of Brother Lawrence, the testimony of Saint Francis and innumerable others. The prophetic fellowship is the communal expression of this lay work of reflection and biblical understanding.

The Role of Theological Specialists

This prophetic fellowship obviously raises many questions about the role of the religious professional or clergyman. What is the task of the theologically trained specialist in a secularized world?

No full answer can be given to such a question until such time as the servant Church takes much fuller shape as the prophetic fellowship. Nevertheless, a foreshadowing of the role of the religious professional is already discernible. At present, the clergyman is trained as a theological specialist and yet works as a personal counselor and administrative expert. This is the contradiction inherent in theological training within our secularized world. Theological schools are torn two ways by this situation, for they wish to make the theological training more relevant, and yet they are convinced that a clergyman should be trained primarily for theological reflection and preaching. In the present structure, this is an insoluble dilemma. If, on the other hand, the laity are the apostolate of the Church, then we need clergy or religious specialists who are theologically prepared to give time and attention to working with laity. This means that preaching, personal care, cultic activity and administrative work would take a very secondary place in the work of the theological specialists. Preaching in the worldly structures, where it occurs, would be a layman's task. The clergyman is primarily needed as a theological resource for this lay apostolate. The layman needs openness to the historical struggles in which he and others are engaged; he needs sufficient theological depth to recognize that he is always over his depth when reflecting on the mysteries of man's existence in history. The servant Church implies, therefore, a new conception of the office of the religious specialist; it calls for a very different conception of theological training.

At present, men prepare for the role of religious specialist as though they were to be *the ministers* of the Church. At every step of their preparation from the initial struggle to share in a private language up to the donning of special clothes or a peculiar liquidity of intonation, the religious specialist is separated from the historical struggle of the world. The prophetic fellowship has no place for such spokesmen for private, religious culture; it desperately needs men who are engaged in the historical struggle rather than fleeing from it; it calls for men and women who are open to history because they have plumbed the depths of historical encounter in the light of the saving history. The prophetic fellowship needs theological specialists in a way that other forms of the Church in other periods of history never needed them, for it works with a theologically self-conscious laity. However, the Church in a secular world needs specialists who are willing to be auxiliary aids to the laity rather than attempting to enlist the laity as auxiliaries to their organizational enterprise.

Another difficult question about the prophetic fellowship is whether this understanding of apostolate has any roots among the laity. If the servant Church is really the present life of the Church as it begins to manifest itself in the emerging society, we should expect to find laymen already serving in it or ready to share its life. This is, indeed, the case; in fact, many more laymen than clergy are searching for this authentic ministry. Consider, for example, the following letter from a layman to his pastor:

"Recently I have been mulling a problem over in my mind. A problem that may not have an answer.

[94]

In fact it may not really be a problem at all. None the less I have attempted to discuss the problem-feeling with others, and as a good many things are, it was hard to seriously express in words, the feeling you were attempting to convey. It's even harder to lay down the self erected barriers of society and seriously give vent to your very personal feelings; and thus my discussions were on the light side but a feeling was conveyed.

"Basically the problem centers around a feeling of unfulfillment—if there is such a word. Many of us have reached an age where the children are no longer very young and demanding. Our incomes while not high are reasonable and we've learned to live within them. We have the stoves, refrigerators, washing machines, homes, cars, etc., that our standard of living requires. Our job, while interesting, no longer takes one hundred per cent of our available time and we realize we're in all probability, not going to be President, Senator, or a personage of State or National importance.

"Now we have time to stop running after the elusive target. We can walk at a brisk pace, but we can walk. We have the precious commodity of time but we are unfulfilled. In former years a man would carve a home, with his hands, out of the woods. He had a feeling, an intangible feeling, of accomplishment. Today this is not done. The man of yesteryear would leave his mark for the generations that came after him. Today man earns money and buys his needs and a basic unfulfillment comes into being.

"It's true we leave our children and they reflect parental influence. In our employment we try and do more than is required, because of an honest interest and desire to be worthy of our hire. We have many acquaintances and a lesser number of friends. But this is not sufficient to give the feeling of accomplishment or fulfillment that is necessary.

"Perhaps this letter does not properly reflect its true meaning. It is not intended as a letter of complaint or of dis-satisfaction. It is intended to pose a question as to what a man can do; and how he goes about doing it; to acquire a feeling that what he is doing, or should be doing, is for a purpose, a worthy purpose that will give him the quiet satisfaction of knowing that he has done something, or is doing something, that is unselfishly worth while?"

This letter is obviously not typical, for each man comes to his encounter with historical responsibility in his own way. Nevertheless, for anyone who has worked in the lay movement, this is a very characteristic concern of men and women in all classes of society and among all groups; all of us are asking about the meaning of our lives. Many Christians today are ready for service or sacrifice. They fear only the emptiness and despair that plague a life which is preoc-

cupied with desire and gain. They are asking about
the meaning of the present in the light of the future.
Perhaps this is the note which is sounded in an affluent
society or at a certain stage of technological development. However, it seems a more profound and universal note than that, for it is to be heard in the most
underdeveloped as well as the most overdeveloped
areas of the world. Men and women are asking about
their responsibility for the future and the society
which they are called to create. They are free from
fear of mysterious powers in a nether world. They
know that they belong to a human interdependence
which requires their commitment and sacrifice. Many
of them are ready for these sacrifices, but the churches
seem to divert them into organizational loyalty and encourage them merely to be industrious in their occupational activities. Organizational loyalty is not responsibility for the history in which we are engaged,
although certain kinds of loyalty are required and
fostered in every community. Occupation is certainly
a sphere of obedience and a place of ministry, but
sheer diligence in a meaningless round of occupational
activities is neither ministry nor salvation. Terms such
as "vocation" or "stewardship" avoid these basic questions; in fact stewardship is little more than a fund-
raising "gimmick" in most churches. Up to this time,
the churches have been content to say, "Be loyal and
be diligent in your work," but this avoids the serious
problems that men and women are facing today.

People are asking about their salvation; they would

not phrase the question this way, but that is the real meaning of the letter which has just been read. The question is asked today in terms of the meaning of life. It asks what future there may be which gives meaning and form to our present decisions and existence. It asks for the ultimate meaning which shapes the penultimate sacrifice. It asks about history and the depth of its commitments and sacrifices. This is the question of salvation in a secularized world. The prophetic fellowship is the Church's openness to this question of meaning in the secular world. The apostolate of the laity is participation with the world in reflection on these searching questions—to share out of faith in the troubling doubt which such questions evoke. The Church as cultic body or confessional assembly creates no scandal in a secular world, for these religious forms offer escapes from a secular history rather than judgments within a secular world. The prophetic fellowship opens secular history itself to questions of ultimate meaning, disclosing both the scandal and the promise of the saving history.

THE NEW CREATION AS METROPOLIS

CHAPTER IV

The Ministry of Communication

When we ask about the ministry of the servant
Church, we are asking about the embodiment of the
prophetic fellowship as servanthood of the laity; we
are also asking how this embodiment is related to the
world's struggle. Even as the prophetic fellowship carries out its apostolate in the midst of the world's struggle to shape its future, it exercises its ministry in the
context of the broken relationships of the world. The
Church as cultic society exercised its ministry by re-
placing the disorder of the world with its order. The
Church as confessing fellowship embodied a sanctified
life within its elect community and exercised its obedience in the world. The Church as servanthood of the

laity is the discernment of the New Mankind within the structures of the world's life.

The secular world experiences a crisis of meaning as it discovers its historical responsibility; the shape of the future becomes problematical and the image of what a man is meant to be becomes blurred. This crisis over the shape of the future expresses itself in preoccupation with the problem of goals. When the future becomes problematical, scholars reflect upon the rise and fall of cultures; every human project is bracketed with an "if"; a sense of uncertainty hangs over the most trivial occasions; nations feel a summons of destiny and yet plunge after that destiny as though fearful that it will elude them. The foundations are truly shaken, for mankind experiences a profound restlessness when it loses assurance about the future.

A crisis of the future is brought on by a breakdown in the unity of a society, and yet such a crisis of meaning is itself a cause of further disruption in the coherence of life. When men become uncertain about their sense of direction, even though it be a sense of direction of which they were never particularly conscious, they experience a certain *malaise*. We see this mood in the youth of the United States, if not throughout the Western world. Such generalizations are, of course, difficult to validate, and yet the nostalgic return to folk music among American youth and the extreme form of *malaise* in the beatnik movement suggest a loss of confidence in the future among the younger generation. The paths marked out by the parents no longer offer challenge or promise. The very content of what it means to be a success is called into question. A certain ennui, a kind of marking time, and in many cases a simple resignation to suburban conformity are the more obvious symptoms of this crisis of meaning. Life seems to be in fragments; the pieces no longer make a coherent pattern. The universe of meaning dissolves; birth, marriage, a job, community responsibility and political responsibility seemed to make some kind of whole, but now each of these activities becomes an unrelated chore; indeed, merely fulfilling these expectations requires ever greater effort. A crisis of meaning is symptomatic of the breakdown in the motivational power and coherence of a society; it is, at the same time, a causal force in the further disorganization of a society.

Broken Communication

We experience the disorganization of American society largely as a breakdown of communication. This disruption of communication is not necessarily bad, to be sure, since it is a sign that men are seeking new modes of interdependence, even as the crisis in meaning is a sign that men are no longer content with the economic values that have dominated American life. Nevertheless, the breakdown of communication is intimately related to the loss of a sense of meaning and direction, for the universe of discourse among men depends upon a common world of meaning. The most obvious and much discussed example of the break-down of communication is the university campus of the United States. The university is no longer a *university* since there is no common world of meanings through which communication is mediated; there is no *universe*. Disruption of communication character-izes the various fields within social science, for ex-ample, as much as it does the relationships between the humanities, the human sciences and the physical sci-ences. The preoccupation with linguistic communica-tion in philosophy today, however abstract it may seem at times, reflects an attempt to overcome the wide-spread disruption of communication. Moreover, the experience of the university can be duplicated in the relationships between persons, social classes, racial groups and social structures within the society. We are experiencing a crisis of the person, of the com-munity, and above all of public responsibility. To this extent, the university offers a parable of our world.

Evidences of the disruption of communication are present everywhere in urban life. The most obvious sign is the growing schism between central cities and suburban areas: we have one world of inner city depri-vation and another world of suburban affluence. There is less and less encounter between these groups in the informal atmosphere of residential association. The United States, despite its long-standing pride in its open class system, is rapidly developing a caste system in its metropolitan areas. These walls of separation in the metropolitan structure are reinforced by dislocations in the communal fabric of neighborhoods and local communities.

Juvenile crime is a dramatic symptom of this disrupted communication in neighborhoods, for the young respond to disorder in their framework of expectations by striking out against the symbols of social obligation; they confirm their sense of alienation from human community by shattering the external pretense of communication—law and order—to which the world clings. A somewhat less dramatic but even more serious breakdown of communication has developed between the communal areas and their so-called political representatives. This vacuum between political decision-making and local community is intimately related to the disruption of communication in local communities, but it also reflects the loss of communication between residential areas and the field of public responsibility. The politics of local communities become a first line of defense against public responsibility rather than a source of responsible participation in the building of metropolis.

Many causal factors can be adduced for the disruption of communication in metropolitan life. Our immediate concern, however, is to indicate the field of ministry in which the servant Church expresses its life in the emerging metropolis. The ministry of reconciliation of the servant Church is the restoration of communication to society. *Love, in this sense, is open communication, and the ministry of love is the re-opening of communication.* The apostolate proclaims

[103]

the reality of the New Mankind in the historical forms of thought appropriate to a secular world. The ministry embodies this New Mankind as reopened communication in metropolis. The ministry of the prophetic fellowship is the embodiment of the love to which it witnesses.

The task of ministry is never general, although it embodies a universal human identity in particular communal forms. The New Mankind is embodied amid the alienations of a particular society. The work of ministry enters concretely into the disruption in communication as the field of its reconciling work. The apostolate of the prophetic fellowship assumes the form of historical reflection which is congruent with the universe of meaning in a secular society. The ministry of reconciliation undertakes the task of opening communication between persons and structures in a metropolitan world.

The ministry of reconciliation comprehends the whole scope of broken communication in our world, and especially the penetration of the wall that separates East from West; consequently, our concern with metropolis is only exemplary of the total task of ministry in the world today. This ministry proclaims and embodies a universal identity which is concretely expressed in various societies and yet transcends the national and ideological boundaries which separate these societies.

We speak here of apostolate and ministry as though they were discrete processes in the servant Church, but

[104]

this manner of speaking serves only to clarify the distinct responsibilities of the Church in the world. These processes of reflection and communication are actually inseparable, for a witnessing fellowship is a ministering body and a ministering community is a witnessing Church. Apostolate has occasionally been sundered from the prophetic fellowship, but then it represents unconscious or latent membership in the New Mankind. All men share in the reality of the New Mankind, for this is their essential manhood, the community to which they belong in Christ. They may, in fact, affirm this New Mankind without full awareness of its source, but then they attest their humanity and share the apostolate of the Church. The work of ministry also occurs outside the orbit of the believing apostolate, but then ministry is unwitting embodiment of the New Mankind. The Church as conscious witness to man's true being can affirm every apostolate and ministry in which the New Mankind finds faithful expression. However, the distinctive task of the servant Church is to express the unity of apostolate and ministry both within the structure of its own life and in the acknowledgment of the New Mankind within the historical structures of society.

Apostolate and ministry are also united through participation in a common understanding of the world; at least, the Church's proclamation is coherently expressed when apostolate and ministry issue from such a common ground. *Proclamation as historical reflection and ministry as communication find their common*

ground in the interpersonal understanding of reality.
Man is who he is in relationship to other persons; his
being is a co-being. The discovery of one's own identity, what we mean by individuality of the person, is a
process of reflection or self-consciousness within the
network of communication and community. My consciousness of who I am, my personal being, is thus
mediated to me in communication with others and as
a consequence of reflection upon myself in the light
of the responses I evoke in others. This interpersonal
world is the substratum upon which reflection and
communication rest.

The relationship of reflection to communication can
be illustrated by considering what it means to be a
father. A man carries out many tasks within a family,
however well or poorly, and he wins a certain standing
as father of his children. His being a father, however,
is only very secondarily a question of his being the
physiological parent of his children; we recognize the
personal character of fatherhood, for example, in view-
ing the father of adopted children in the same way that
we view what is called a natural father. Furthermore,
being a father is not even something which a man can
achieve, although he has to fulfill many obligations to
place himself in the situation where he may be called
a father. The full sense of identity as father can only
be bestowed upon a person by his children when they
address him as Father. The identity which he has assumed as a task must in time be given to him as a gift.
He is ultimately dependent upon others for who he is

in the world; they mediate an identity to him. At some point, when his fourteen-year-old comes to him and penetrates the inhibitions and barriers of communication, calling him father and treating him as father by asking his counsel as son-to-father, then he discovers the depth of the meaning of being as the father of his child. He is held, thus, in his being in the world through a network of recognition and response which we call communication. He is never, however, an integral part of this network except as he discloses himself within this community; this is his freedom, his distance from all external domination. Moreover, he always has his own distance from himself in this network, and his reflection upon the responses of others to his own disclosures gives him his understanding of himself within this world. His consciousness becomes self-consciousness or self-identity. His historicity, his question about the meaning of being in the world, is inseparable from the interpersonal world in which he becomes conscious of himself. The network of open communication is the medium of the reflective process through which persons come to be in the world.

Reflection and communication are not only inseparably bound together through their common ground in the interpersonal world; they are also the categories of understanding appropriate to a historical interpretation of man's being in the world. We have already considered the historicity of man's being which comes into prominence in a secular world; now we see the interpersonal character of the world of historical man.

Man asks about the problem of meaning, because he knows himself to be dependent upon his decisions and projects within an interpersonal world of address and response. The reflective process through which a father, for example, considers his identity as a father, stems from the historical question about the meaning of his being in the world. If the duties of fatherhood are ritualized and prescribed, his task is to conform to this ritualized set of expectations. His son is that person toward whom such and such obligations are due. However, when the traditional structure of a society is disrupted and the interpersonal world becomes a sphere of decisions, the parent constitutes his obligations in the light of the address and response of the other person. He is constantly being pressed to ask who this other person is and who he is in this relationship. The problem of identity becomes paramount. Ultimately, he is pressed to ask about the meaning of his actions not only for the future of this other person but also for his own significance as a person.

The fixed obligations which label other persons with unchanging identities collapse in a complex society, raising the question of meaning and opening the network of the interpersonal world to reflection. When the interpersonal world is taken seriously as the field of decision and creative response, man has moved into the historical mode of conceiving his world according to its possibilities and his own responsibility. Personal responsibility cannot be transferred to an external set of obligations or attributed to the threat of punishment from outside; indeed, the degeneration of the personal world into reliance upon external obligation is what we mean by pathology in an interpersonal world of human responsibility and freedom. Historical man is the man who finds himself freed to answer responsibly for his identity in the world; he knows that his answer to the meaning of being in the world is bound up with the interpersonal world which mediates this identity to him. To take an extreme example, the identity of the white man in the United States is dependent upon the way the Negro sees him and how he understands the Negro. His identity and the meaning of his life are inextricably bound up with this interpersonal world through which he receives his identity, even as his history is decisively determined by his decisions for or against this neighbor in the interpersonal world.

The interpersonal world is never, to be sure, a totally unstructured world in which being a father, for example, is simply constituted by the arbitrary decisions of each person. The important roles in every society have a certain structure, and there is a point of zero tolerance at which one ceases to fulfill the role. At the point at which a father ceases to support his family, deliberately deserting them, the public and the courts would consider him bound by the obligations of a father but not acting like a father. The difference between the traditional world and the secularized world of historical man is, therefore, primarily a difference in interpretation of obligations. In the traditional world, man knows himself to be bound to nature, his social relationships and the superworld of mythic or demonic powers through a set of fixed obligations. Whatever flexibility may be allowed in the fulfillment of these obligations, departure from this ordered world can only bring punishment and destruction. Freedom is essentially the power to conform to these obligations. The free man is the one who is motivated to do his duty. This world of obligations loses its fixity with the development of science, technology and industry, for change replaces tradition as the dominant principle of society. The world is disenchanted, as Max Weber expressed it. Man finds himself responsible for his world and to a large extent responsible for the character of the social and cultural world of which he is a part. He is no longer simply a part to be conformed to the world; he is the creator of a world for which he is answerable. This is the rise of historical consciousness in which freedom is not only meeting the obligations of the interpersonal world but also answerability for creating that world and its meanings through responses and decisions. Freedom is the "courage to be"—the courage to assume responsibility for one's future.

Historical understanding is, therefore, much more than a device for talking about the ultimate in a secular world. Historical categories are the truly human terms. Man's understanding of himself and his world are mediated in the interpersonal matrix for which he is responsible; this responsibility is what it means to have a history and be a person, for the identity disclosed in our reflection is mediated through our communion with others. Thus, reflection and communication emerge as the categories in which a secular age will appropriate its past, consider its true humanity and face its ultimate commitment.

When we recognize that human reality is interpersonal, which is to say that man's being in the world can be understood ultimately as address and response, we can interpret sin as refusal of response and damnation as exclusion from response. If we understand freedom as capacity to respond, the *power to be* within the interpersonal network of address and response, we can also conceive the misuse of freedom as the attempt to control the other's response, treating him or her as an object of one's manipulations rather than a free subjectivity. This is denial of one's own dependence upon the response of the other person—denial of his belonging in that interworld of human interdependence; it is thus denial of one's own humanity as dependent. Being in the world as a person, on the other hand, is living with the freedom of the other person—acknowledging his humanity and simultaneously one's own personhood. To reject the anxiety of this world of freedom for an illusory world under one's own control is to cut oneself off from response by obliterating the very subjectivity which would give that response. This exclusion from response is damnation, and is a work which *man does* through his refusal of response and exercise of domination. The tragedy of Little Rock, Arkansas, Ole Miss and Deerfield, Illinois, inheres in the self-imposed damnation of these communities, since their refusal of recognition to the Negro is a way of excluding themselves from the world.

The world of broken communication, where domination, exploitation, stereotype, prejudice and hatred reign, is the world in which the servant Church recalls men to their true being as the New Mankind of freedom and response. The ministry of reconciliation is, therefore, principally a work of listening and invoking response. In the final analysis, this ministry invokes the kind of world in which respect of persons, equality of access to the world and freedom of participation in the community are ensured, for it seeks to establish the conditions of open communication; indeed, the servant Church knows that social structure is needed to assure *the conditions* for interpersonal existence but cannot guarantee *the substance* of the New Mankind. For this reason, the servant Church works for political change without becoming a political party. The ministry of reconciliation is the laity opening the world to the reality of the New Mankind and calling the world to reshape its structures according to this reality.

The ministry of reconciliation is not, to be sure, merely the attempt by a religious institution to implement a program of social reform, although social reform is a consequence of its ministry. The Church's task is to carry on her apostolate and ministry within the historical struggle; the presence of the New Mankind is mediated in the historical struggle through this ministering fellowship, so that its call to reflection is simultaneously a mediation of the power for open communication. The New Mankind, as the opening of communication, is present wherever recognition and response establish a network of community. Open communication is the presence of the New Mankind as personal response. Restating the *saving events* in this metaphor of communication, we can affirm that the Covenant is the reopening of communication between God and man—God's *recognition* of man; the Resurrection is the continuity of this divine recognition amid man's refusal of response; the Church discloses this triumph as living response; the reconciling ministry is the Church's mediation of this divine recognition within the world's alienations. Thus, open communication and the New Mankind come together as the interpersonal reality in which human life and human history find their fulfillment. Open communication is the New Mankind in history as love. The presence of the New Mankind is deliverance from the fear that forecloses the future: man creates his identity in commitment to this New Mankind even as he receives his identity in recognition by the New Mankind. Hence, the New Mankind is never a program of social reform nor an institutional project of the religious enterprise; it is always *a presence* in which men participate and through which they discover the meaning of their lives.

The Pastorate in Metropolitan Society

The ministry of the Church embodies the commitment to the New Mankind. This ministry seeks to evoke personal community and to establish structures in society within which communication is maintained. This is the real meaning of the pastorate of the Church, for pastorate is sustaining the open communication of the New Mankind within the arena of human struggle and alienation. The New Mankind is the true humanity of all men; thus, the Church is the community which is conscious of this identity and committed to its presence in the world. The servant Church affirms the sustaining of life and communication by foremen, shop stewards, teachers, mothers, political leaders and others. This ministry of preservation of life is primarily a lay task in a secularized world. The maintenance of open communication discloses the New Mankind as pastorate.

The breakdown of communication manifests itself initially as a crisis in personal identity. Consequently, the ministry of reconciliation means first a ministry of listening, of attentiveness to the personal search for significant response. This search for intimacy is probably the most obvious symptom of the disruption of communication in contemporary life. Here again, the beatnik movement offers an illuminating example of the crisis, for the beatnik surrenders the search for meaning, and yet the beatnik engages in an endless search for response from the other person; he is looking for himself in the other's response. Albert Camus penetrated to the heart of this contemporary sickness in his book *The Fall;* he depicts the despair of a man who discovers his incapacity to respond to the call of another person—the lonely call for help of a young woman drowning in a canal. The crisis of the person today is a search for response by one who is unable to respond.

The ministry of the prophetic fellowship addresses itself first to a restructuring of many aspects of our society, for the crisis of the person is created primarily by the domination of economic values in all spheres of life. The conditions of stable, communal life do not resolve the search for personal identity, but they form the network of stable responses in which the person can pursue this search creatively. Human community rather than economic exploitation will have to receive first consideration. At present, our unstable communal life is generating far more personal disorder than can be treated by the skilled ministries of psychiatrist and professional pastor. The medical offices and churches are crowded with people who are experiencing serious mental and emotional disturbances. The personal crisis in our society is interdependent with the communal crisis which is so manifest in the metropolitan neighborhoods. In American society, every phase of personal community is undergoing a radical disruption under the weight of economic standards of success. Consider the teen-age culture, the interracial relationships, the zoning of residential communities against social and racial differences, the stress experienced in almost every home between husband and wife and between parents and children. In all of these communal groups we are seeing serious dislocations whose principal source is the struggle on the ladder of success.

Various rationalizations are offered for this state of affairs by those who feel called to justify the American way of life. These rationalizations are usually irrelevant, for most of them maintain either that life has always been this way, which is sheer nonsense, or that the productivity and freedom of the American way of life exact a certain price in communal integrity. These justifications really amount to a defense of the domination of economic exploitation over the human values of the society. Inevitably certain dislocations will follow upon technological change in production; this is the dynamic aspect of a society which applies technology to its environment. However, the subordination of communal and public life to the unpredictable effects of technological dislocation represents an abdication of responsibility for the future of society.

The churches are attempting to cope with the crisis of person and community largely through the pastorate of the clergymen to individuals; indeed, many clergy are now very skilled in the field of counseling and provide a free service which is comparable to some of the best psychological counseling. However, the increasing demand for personal attention and the lack of communal structures in which men and women can find a healthy interpersonal environment create a *cul de sac* for the clergy and the churches. The clergyman has very few institutional controls to protect him in counseling relationships; meanwhile the churches become leaderless as clergy are diverted to endless individual cases. Of course, the clergy are attracted to this counseling role because they have a kind of "Catcher in the Rye" complex and feel significant as helpers of the weak. This is very treacherous ground, however, since personal entanglement in these deeper, psychological disturbances is all but inevitable without the controls of regular office hours, set fees and associated professional advice at regular intervals.

One can only respect the devotion and skill with which the clergy are carrying on this personal pastorate today, for the crisis in person and community deepens with each passing decade. If the preceding interpretation seems to devalue this pastoral contribution, it is only as a judgment upon the futility of siphoning the efforts of the clergy into this field. Whatever course the churches take, the ministry of reconciliation requires a willingness to listen and be attentive to the invocation for response. This applies, of course, to clergymen as well as to the ministering laity. However, the opening of communication is a much deeper and more difficult task than the diversion of our theological specialists into personal counseling. The clergymen cannot *be* the pastorate of the Church; their present attempt to be this pastorate eventuates in their own destruction and obstructs the reopening of communication in the society.

The ministry of opening communication means the reorganization of American society in the light of the New Mankind. It is appalling to contemplate the scope of this task, but it is simply ingenuous to see this ministry on any smaller scale. Moreover, this ministry of reconciliation cannot be effected through power politics, for it is only ministry as it awakens people to their true calling and responsibility for the future of this society and our world. We cannot outline the full scope of this ministry here, but its central thrust should be denoted.

The reorganization of American society is some of the unfinished business of our domestic world; this is a task which we Americans have thus far avoided. The metropolitan expansion and the change in the character of American communities make it impossible to forego this responsibility any longer.

In the first half of the nineteenth century, the urban areas of the United States and the new areas of settlement experienced radical dislocation. This breakdown occurred in the emerging East coast cities, but it also exploded in the mining areas of the West. One need only reflect on the Vigilante period to realize that sheer chaos had developed in parts of the West. This disorganization was counteracted by the waves of immigration from Europe during the nineteenth century. How ironical it is to think that Congress restricted immigration in the twentieth century on the basis of supposedly scientific reports that the immigrants were filling our jails and asylums, when in fact the immigrants had brought stability to our marital structures, religious life and urban development. To be sure, the poverty and dislocation of many of these people placed them in categories of the population from which high rates of crime and disorganization were to be expected, but no unprejudiced view of the statistics over this long period can miss the fact that membership in an ethnic community was the major stabilizing factor in American community life.

With the dissolution of ethnic communities the stability of communal and religious life has declined rapidly. Central city areas are becoming increasingly a scene of broken neighborhoods, superhighway constructions or mammoth, impersonal housing projects. The virtual cessation of immigration after World War I has brought a radical weakening of ethnic ties after forty years. Ethnic communities today are merely remnants of earlier linguistic and religious communities, for the expanding middle class was replenished from these upwardly mobile and hard-working ethnic groups.

This emerging crisis in communal life is further complicated by strain in the relationships between the in-migrant Negro ethnics and the white ethnic communities. The Negro could have been considered a separate racial group during the period of his original introduction to these shores in the status of a slave, although the real meaning of race is very perplexing when subjected to scientific scrutiny. However that may be, the American Negro, like every other American, represents a particular ethnic group now. Whatever special ethnic traits he possesses, in fact, are largely a consequence of his former status as a slave and the discrimination which he has experienced subsequently at the hands of other ethnic groups. The American Negro is probably the most American of all ethnics, since his former language and culture were stamped out in the period of slavery and his actual culture is in every respect authentically American. Nevertheless, the Negro lacks the solidarity of former ethnic in-migrants, for he lacks the linguistic and cultural uniqueness of the alien ethnic; moreover, his own culture is disrupted by the internal tensions created by the discrimination which he has experienced. An American identity should be the Negro's greatest asset; however, it becomes a temporary liability in his attempt to adjust from a discriminatory situation to first-class citizenship in the metropolitan area. Furthermore, other ethnic groups fear a loss of status from contact with Negro ethnics; consequently, additional tensions aggravate the internal disruption of the Negro community.

One further aspect of this communal situation illuminates the direction in which the reorganizing task of the laity will have to move. The breakdown of the ethnic communities leaves the urban areas with the unfinished business which they were beginning to face in the first half of the nineteenth century. We can no longer postpone the organization of a metropolitan society in which human values are respected and cultural achievements find their true place. However, the sphere of public responsibility has also been impoverished by the dissolution of ethnic ties. The ethnic communities exercised a steady pressure upon the public sphere according to their particular stage of development in American life. If one looks back upon the political formations of our great cities, it is clear that these ethnic communities have taken their turn in guiding the course of urban development as they reached the second and third generation of their tenure. Now a gap in public responsibility emerges from the breakdown of ethnic identities. Unstable urban communities provide little direct pressure on their so-called representatives and in turn exact very little recognition from the higher echelons of the metropolitan bureaucracy. Meanwhile middle-class leadership has taken flight into small-town politics in the suburban communities, leaving the metropolitan center to its own devices. The Negro ethnics are beginning to take some responsibility for central city politics, but the wealthier segments of the metropolitan community have withdrawn support and leadership from the orbit of city politics. At the very moment when our large cities face the task of urban organization, financial resources and personal leadership have been withdrawn.

This state of affairs seems far removed from the crisis of persons with which we started this consideration of communal problems: nevertheless, the person is "who he is" through the mediation of his interpersonal world, and the pastorate addresses itself as much to his interpersonal environment as to his immediate, personal needs. The ministry of reconciliation is the exercise of the pastorate over this broad range of problems; its essential thrust is for the organization of a metropolitan society. Once the clergy realize that pastorate cannot be restricted to shepherding the cultic body or maintaining the confessional assembly, they will also understand that they cannot preempt the pastorate from the laity.

The Church as *confessional assembly* maintained its pastorate as a kind of chaplaincy to the ethnic community; meanwhile, the ethnic community exercised the pastorate of public responsibility through its political engagements in city life. The Church as *cultic body* exercised its pastorate through the establishment of a coalition with the princes; thus, the cultic Church sustained its personal discipline and informed the maintenance of order. The cultic and confessional types of pastorate are not viable in a metropolitan society. The Church as confessional assembly ceased to be an adequate form when it lost its local base in the ethnic community. Every attempt to work from the confessional assembly today degenerates into a social class church which is segregated from public responsibility. The opening of communication in metropolitan areas calls for a servanthood of the laity within the public spheres of responsibility; thus, it requires the creation of structures in which laity can find training and support for the ministry of communication.

The Church faces several fronts on which communication needs to be opened and interpersonal community realized. The churches are quite aware that they have been relatively ineffective in the task of racial desegregation. The servanthood of the laity calls for a reflective, planned, long-range program for the racial integration of our metropolitan areas. The same applies to the social class barriers that are steadily growing in our cities; indeed, the opening of communication across social class lines may prove even more difficult than overcoming ethnic tensions between Negro and white. This task of reconciliation can be accomplished only through the planning and development of politically responsible local communities throughout the metropolitan area. Hence, the community of the servant Church has to be seriously engaged in the struggle for local community, and yet it has to be organized as a fellowship which finds its true citizenship in metropolis. The ministry of reconciliation has, therefore, the task of stabilizing local communities as open communities rather than ghettoes, and yet helping the members of these local communities to discover their true identity as citizens of metropolis. The local church as confessional assembly, preoccupied with the cultivation and nurture of its own membership, misses the real thrust of this embodiment of the New Mankind. The true pastorate is ministry of the laity *in* the secular world; it mediates the power and vision of the New Mankind in the disrupted processes of metropolitan communication.

New Forms of the Church

Several new religious structures are needed to sustain the ministry of reconciliation under the pressures of metropolitan struggle. The chaplaincies to local communities are anchored in local congregations; however, this religious form needs a broader base; it has to become a lay center for theological training of the laity and for cultivation of public responsibility. Such lay centers are needed in suburban areas even more than they are needed in the disrupted communities of the inner city. In the suburban area, such centers can develop only through painstaking effort, since the suburbanite is clinging desperately to a world which he thinks he possesses. Lay centers concerned with racial integration, incorporation of the suburb into metropolitan responsibility, and attention to the control of zoning and taxation on behalf of metropolis will pose a much greater threat in the suburb than within the inner city.

There is a concerted effort today to organize inner city communities as racial and factional power groups which can exploit the political vulnerability of the city for the sake of local gain. The emergence of this kind of power organization, usually called a "community organization," is very appealing to inner city clergy who feel helpless to elicit the support of the churches or the political leaders to meet the desperate needs of inner city communities. Here again, a lay center can strengthen the hand of the laity and the theological specialists; such a center can facilitate limited cooperation with power groups and encourage the development of political responsibility in the local communities.

Residential centers will have to be secondary to the evangelical centers in which the ministry to public administration, health and welfare, metropolitan planning and industrial life can be sustained. Public ministries are prior in our world. Whether one or many centers will prove to be the most suitable for such ministries can be learned only through the development of this servanthood of the laity. Clearly the laity need help from theological specialists; they need help in problems of counseling, development of an understanding of group processes and insight in grasping the scope of the metropolitan and political development of our world. Furthermore the ministry to industrial groups will undoubtedly become increasingly difficult as the prophetic fellowship awakens the need for increased planning. Nevertheless, this is all the more reason for the creation of industrial missions which open communication within industrial life and between the leadership of labor and management and the public structures of our society.

We have seen that the Church undertook the Christianizing of the Western world through a *cultic form.* In the medieval period Western society was dominated by the structures of familial life and blood kinship; an organic form of society and a cultic expression of the Church converged to embody the New Mankind as a mystical organism. The Church then delivered Western society from control by religious authority through the protest of the confessional assembly; this protest secularized public responsibility; this secularization was effected, moreover, by gathering the familial community independently of the productive forces which were shaping the development of Western society. Church and society developed as co-existent forces, creating a dual focus of inner community of faith and external productive society. We are entering an era of social coherence and international community in which the productive forces of science and technology will be directed on behalf of national and international stability. We have left the familial and productive eras; we have embarked upon a political phase of Western history. This new era need not bring a collectivization of life, although the collective development of the largest portion of the globe indicates that the coordinative forces are becoming dominant in the world. History has to be changed as well as grasped. Whatever forms the structures of government, planning and public administration assume in the emerging metropolis, neither the Church as cultic body nor the Church as confessional assembly can sustain a ministry of communication within these structures. The forms of proclamation, ministry and pastorate gain their authenticity through their embodiment of the saving history in the historical struggle of the society in which they are placed. The new era of metropolis calls for forms of the Church which can proclaim and embody the New Mankind *within* the structures of this new world. Thus, the evangelical centers and academies will not be auxiliaries to the residential churches; they will be the Church in the new society.

The most disturbing experience for church members in our time is to find their confessional assemblies divided over public and economic issues. Men and women today look to the local congregation as a haven from conflict and tension. Clergymen view their work as the maintenance of harmonious relationships within the flock; the frictionless machine is the ideal image of the congregation. The creation of such *harmonious enclaves* is an indication of the utter dislocation of the Church in our society. The Church is intended to be a *suffering body* in the world, showing forth the Lord's death until He come. This community in Christ is not called to sacrifice its ministry of reconciliation in order to preserve its inner tranquillity. This body is called to bear within itself the sufferings imposed upon it by a ministry of reconciliation within the broken communication of the world. Reopening broken communication will inevitably tear and disrupt the internal life of the Church, but that inner suffering is the essential nature of the authentic presence of the New Mankind in the world. The work of the clergyman is not to spare the ministering fellowship from internal suffering by diverting it from its ministry; his task is to open new possibilities of ministry to which the servant Church is summoned, deepening the reflection of the prophetic fellowship in the course of its sufferings. There is no Church without such a ministry.

If the Church creates chaplaincies, lay centers and training academies in place of local congregations, many clergymen and laymen wonder what becomes of the preaching and sacramental life which have been such prominent features of the confessional and cultic forms of the Church. We have already noted that the cultic and confessional moments are always present in human existence and will always be marks of the total expression of the Church's mediation of the New Mankind. The cultic moment is present because the Church's identity in the world involves a continuity with the past; her future as the New Mankind is eternally present through the divine initiative. This tie of future to past is mediated through *forms* which point to an eternal being or identity, yet they take on new concrete expressions in each particular age. The Eucharist mediates this eternal identity as the New Mankind, yet its concrete expression in the prophetic fellowship becomes a communion of the laity in their Lord's suffering through the sharing of His ministry in the world. The recollective act of Eucharistic participation finds a new setting in the world. Eucharist in the setting of reopening communication is a mediation of the communion of man and God which is promised in the New Mankind, for the opening of communication *is* the creation of community whose true depth is participation in the New Mankind. The cultic moment takes on new richness in the servant Church, for it becomes the expression of the servanthood of the laity in the historical struggle for man's humanity as interpersonal being. We have frozen the cultic moment in the congregational assembly. When the cultic life of the servant Church becomes integral to the ministry of the laity, we shall see celebration of the Lord's Supper in the contexts of our communal life. At present, those who are committed to the New Mankind are moving very circumspectly in searching out ways to express an authentic cultic life.

Preaching played such a central role in the confessional assembly that it is inconceivable that its place should become secondary. Nevertheless, preaching will have to become more integral to the tasks of apostolate and pastorate. Critics of the church say that clergymen do not care enough about preaching, are not adequately prepared or lack an appreciation of the Bible. Most of these observations are untrue. The confessional assembly simply provides an impoverished setting for preaching. The work of preaching is to maintain the relationship of the present identity of the Church with the saving events of its foundation; it mediates the true being of the present moment as *trust*. The recounting of the saving events, their interpretation in terms of the contemporary situation and the illumination of the New Mankind in the light of these events: this proclamation testifies to the grounding of the present in the source of all being. Without preaching in this sense the church is assimilated to the world, for it confuses its own hopes with the source of all hope, the source of being itself. In the prophetic fellowship, much of this work will have to be carried on through group processes of biblical reflection. This is a type of exposition of Scripture which is appropriate to the servant Church, for it sets the task of reflection within the historical life of the lay community. Certainly, informal preaching will become an essential part of the apostolate of the laity, but communities of biblical reflection can also create a new environment for preaching. The great assembly and the prominent pulpit may never return as expressions of the Church, but such assemblies may emerge as expressions of the interdependence of humanity in metropolis.

The ministry of communication, like the lay apostolate, calls for a new understanding of the nature and task of the Church. Our reflections on these new forms are further complicated by the denominational division of Christianity. The task of reopening communication falls more heavily on the internal life of the churches than upon the society itself. No problem confronting the pastorate of the servant Church can be conceived as a denominational problem; indeed, the denominational question distorts the real issue of ministry in the world. The emerging society wrestles with problems which cut across denominational divisions and even move beyond interfaith rivalries. The prophetic fellowship seeks a reunion of the churches in the work of ministry. Without optimism or pessimism, the prophetic fellowship can work for open communication in metropolis, ministering to the various structures of the society in the name of the New Mankind, uniting in its ministry those of many denominational traditions. The unity of the Church issues from its reality as the ministering presence of the New Mankind in the world; faithful apostolate and obedient pastorate form the authentic witness to this unity in Christ. Such witness is borne in confidence that the broken communication between the churches will ultimately yield to the victory of the New Mankind.

CHAPTER V

The End as Beginning

Throughout these reflections we have contended that
metropolitan man is also historical man—the one who
ponders his future and his personal identity; metropolitan man is the man who raises radical questions about
the meaning of the human enterprise. In theological
language, this is man reflecting on the *Eschaton*—the
Last Things, the End. This historical consciousness has
distant origins, of course, for the nineteenth century
philosophy had already assumed an historical mode;
however, the future was predictable for this period of
historicism and progress; at least, development could
be assumed as an underlying motif in the human enterprise. The historical consciousness of twentieth century man cannot entertain such optimistic notions with

any seriousness. The future has come into radical question, and yet there is no escape from the question of meaning and futurity. The coherence of the world, the unity of human life and the identity of the truly human hinge upon the answers which are given to these reflections on meaning.

We have concerned ourselves rather specifically with the historical consciousness of metropolitan man; consequently, we shall do well to pursue his struggle to this ultimate level of vision and hope. Metropolis is the common world in which metropolitan people can discover their identity and seek fulfillment in hope. Metropolis is the form of the New Creation to which men are summoned; it is the New Creation as social form which we have called the New Mankind. This New Creation is the final or eschatological reality, but its finality is disclosed through the power which it mediates in the historical present; its ultimacy is disclosed in its power as beginning of coherence and unity for metropolitan man. Only as this reality of the New Mankind reconstitutes the historical present of metropolitan man, directing him to the reopening of communication, informing his life with awareness of the humanity to which he belongs—only in this new beginning will metropolis become reality rather than dream. The End is the beginning and source if it is the authentic end of man. The testimony of God's people is that the New Creation to which they belong is, at the same time, the source of their being and existence.

Metropolitan man is drawn away from this vision of reality to an illusory hope for escape from the responsibility for shaping metropolis. The suburban pattern of metropolitan development is symptomatic of this illusion. Suburbia is the image of escape from public responsibility and retirement into the privacy of one's own garden. There are, of course, many practical reasons for the suburban pattern of development—reasons such as the need for space, the technological improvement in transportation and the struggle to avoid tax responsibilities in large urban areas. Nevertheless, many other patterns of residential development could have arisen in the 1920's and 1930's when this suburban process was emerging. To listen to some sociologists, one would think that the suburban pattern was a consequence of fecundity and the gasoline engine; however, the human reality is much more complex than this; men are not simply the automata of instinctual and technological forces. The suburban pattern of development arose as an expression of the American dream—a dream of escape from the oppressive disciplines and massive forces of production, an escape from the public responsibilities of a society whose sheer massiveness had put it beyond the range of comprehension. The suburban development is the illusory vision of escape into small town politics, retreat to the little village of knowing and being known. This pattern of metropolitan development is the major alternative to public responsibility and to the creation of metropolis as a human environment.

[134]

The End as Beginning

The mistake of conscientious people in the central city areas is to assume that this suburban escape is to be blamed only upon those who now live in suburbia; in this way, the onus of responsibility for the degeneration of urban life into a war of all against all can then be blamed upon suburban people and suburban churches. This interpretation of the American reality is a total misunderstanding of the problem. The suburban development is a geographical projection of the American dream; this is the dream which is shared by underprivileged Negroes in the inner city and by blue-collar whites in marginal sections of the central city. The suburban ranch home embodies the retreat of all Americans from public responsibility and commitment to metropolis. The suburban mind is, in fact, often more present in the prejudices, lack of community and inattentiveness to human need which one encounters in the central city. The escape from involvement in the human community is in some ways more fully manifest in the large urban housing developments, for the suburban community is at least a society of children if nothing else. Thus, we misconceive the task of metropolitan man when we attempt to see in the suburban exodus a simple cause of the defeat of metropolis. Suburbia only projects successfully the demonic temptation of man in mass society—the temptation to withdraw to his garden and manicure his private feelings.

The suburban illusion becomes further complicated by the very impetus which it gains after several decades. Once the wealthier segments of the population have withdrawn from the taxable group within the central city, it becomes increasingly difficult to sustain significant values in central city areas; in time, this initial loss is followed by the disappearance of influential churches and institutions. Soon those families who cherish safe play areas for their children and more local responsibility for schools find that suburbia is their logical choice; moreover, the reduction of the tax base soon makes decent urban properties very expensive and families with several children find that it is expedient to live in suburbia, whatever their personal preference. Hence, the suburban dream becomes a powerful force in reshaping the mind and interests of successive generations. This illusion of escape from the organizational society into the private world of small-town politics now becomes a demonic structure which controls the future of the metropolitan area. Therefore, the struggle against the illusions of suburbia, not against the suburbanite nor even the practical arrangements of suburban living, becomes a crucial task in the struggle for metropolis. We now live with the projection of the suburban dream on the landscape; once given this structure, it is crucial to see through the illusions which set it against the metropolitan hope; we need to understand its demonic quality in order to see its potentialities as a source of humanity within the emerging metropolis.

Suburbia is symptomatic of a mass amnesia—a widespread and morbid forgetfulness by which men and women shut out the world of human reality and even the deeper aspects of their own experience. The suburban pattern of residential growth has this morbid quality at its roots, which means that this morbidity runs deeply within the total American culture. We can trace the source of this morbidity to the deep personal alienations that are experienced in a society which has elevated the struggle for economic success to an idolatrous position; however, for our present purposes the character of this mass amnesia is much more important, since this particular shape of the suburban development poses the most serious problems to a human future for man in the metropolitan area.

Social amnesia is perhaps the most striking type of morbid forgetfulness in suburbia. There is a deep forgetfulness of our common humanity, for the suburb is created as a wall against social differences. Suburbia aims at a dead level of sameness which erases any threat of invidious comparison and any uneasiness that one is not doing as well as his neighbor. This externalized conformity makes for shallow association that loses all the richness of the complex human reality. The attempt to erase social differences empties life of its depth and meaning. The believer in the free market excludes a free market in personal encounter; suburbia is the protectionist world *par excellence*. The suburb is an extreme example of social amnesia, reacting with fright and even panic at the thought of racial or social class differences in the residential milieu. The case of Deerfield, Illinois, was most instructive in this respect, for this suburban area reacted with symptoms of hysteria to the possibility of integrated housing in their community. Social amnesia is rejection of the interpersonal reality which we have identified here as the New Mankind—the human community in which all men participate through God's gracious gift.

The suburban image of fulfillment also discloses an occupational amnesia—a flight from any reminders of the productive struggle. Competition on the ladder of success is erased from the suburban screen. Matriarchalism and preoccupation with children are not merely symptomatic of the alienation between residence and work which suburbia has embodied. This feminine domination in suburbia also reflects the attempt to erase every sign of the working, productive life from the privacy of the consumer world. Hostility to work, even morbid rejection of the productive enterprise, can be discerned in this insulation of suburbia against the male world; even the stores have eliminated items of interest to men. Men are no longer really at home in suburbia; they sleep fretfully in this retreat, waiting for the commuter train to take them back to the real world of productivity in which they find their authentic identity. The women too, finally have no home in this retreat, for they are alienated from their mates in such an environment; they too sleep restlessly, if they sleep at all; they too seek release from their isolation through enervating activities or sordid affairs.

The political amnesia of suburbia is perhaps the most damaging and corrupting aspect of this degeneration of the American hope. In this multiplicity of satellite communities we find men and women playing at small-town politics, regretting that national elections do not reflect their conservative hopes, and pretending that they are being politically responsible. Meanwhile, these small-town politicians work to gain tax advantages by placing small industries within their tax areas, and they maintain low costs for their schools by zoning against families who might bring large numbers of children into their communities. These are the politicoes who scorn metropolitan politics as corrupt; these are the citizens who clamor for more superhighways and the destruction of more central city neighborhoods; these are the public-spirited citizenry who rail against public aid and vote down the relief funds which would provide food for underprivileged children. In suburbia the American dream, the hope of fulfillment, degenerates into a conspiracy of public irresponsibility, and all of this is defended in the name of the private values of personal intimacy, care of children and American individualism. Even this much bruited privacy turns out to be superficial conformity. The ideal of the bourgeois marriage in suburbia—the symbol of intimacy—turns out to be

[139]

a hollow sham. Political amnesia is thus fed with illusions which subvert the hope for metropolis and betray the aspirations of its victims.

The churches, needless to say, have profited enormously through their identification with this amnesia. The Church has its essential being in the *anamnesis*, the recollection of God's saving work in Christ; as *Church*, she calls men to their common humanity, to their share in common work, to their common life in public responsibility. The Church betrays her essential nature and the metropolitan peoples when she identifies her task with the provision of public worship for this suburban illusion. The churches now have to ask about the structure of life within which the New Mankind can be embodied and proclaimed. The residential structure is no longer a structure amenable to this proclamation, for it has become the fortress against the New Mankind. These so-called primary structures of life need to be reclaimed for the human community; the residential environment is the most difficult field of mission; its vaunted privacy is shallow and destructive, whereas men need the richness of true privacy and intimacy; its symbolization of personal values is a betrayal of common humanity. However, the mission will have to move from public structures of society to these alienated structures of residence, from the field of production, public life and educational responsibility into the private areas of familial community. The mission cannot move from the private sphere to the public, from the residential congregation to public responsibility. This is an illusion which comes from the outward resemblance of parish or congregation to historic forms of the Church; these forms are now mere shadows, emptied of the substance of the New Creation. The first step in apostolate and ministry, will come in the opening of reflection and communication in the public spheres of life. The work of *anamnesis*, recollection of the true source of our common humanity, can extend from these spheres of public responsibility into the private realm of family and residence. Such a mission to the public spheres of life finds its source and direction in the reality of the New Creation. This reality is set over against the illusion of privacy. The New Mankind comes to us as "the holy city, new Jerusalem, coming down out of heaven from God." This vision is no suburban escape to a private world; from the corruption in a Garden, the human story moves to that dramatic moment of the New Creation, when the divine *recognition* encounters the perfect *response* of trust in Jesus as the Christ. This New Creation in Christ comes to us as our future, our common humanity in Him; it is at the same time creation, for it is the beginning of our life with one another here and now. We can express this vision most fully in the image of the city; the apocalyptic writer used it so and the fathers of the Church after him. The city, or as we have called it, metropolis, is our unity as humanity in the New Creation. This unity is given to us as our future by God's grace; it is given to all and is for all to appropriate and share. No political, economic or religious system controls and allocates this future. Authentic Christianity participates in this common humanity, embodying it before men. Acknowledgment of this reality is the task of the Church in the metropolitan struggle; this witness alone can overcome the morbid forgetfulness of our common humanity which is expressed in the suburban flight. The Church begins its apostolate as prophetic fellowship in wrestling with this demonic power which possesses the American mind; the Church delivers man from the bondage of illusion by mediating to him the reality of his historical responsibility. The renewal of the churches and the renewal of metropolitan life are thus inseparable. The churches face the task of reflection on their true future as the New Mankind; this apostolate engages them simultaneously in the fashioning of metropolis. In receiving this future as their authentic being, they are freed from bondage to the suburban dream of affluence and safety, they are cast into the maelstrom of metropolitan struggle. But these churches are at the same time metropolitan man seeking his true future. He is a man at work in this industry, a woman looking after that home, a teacher struggling to impart some love of learning in that school; man is the Church as the self-consciousness of the New Mankind. Only as this new man appears in obedience, conformed to the true Servant, will metropolitan disintegration turn toward metropolis and the churches become once again mediators of the New Creation. The inseparability of Church and metropolis, God-for-man and man-being-for-man, confronts the churches with their most difficult decision. To be for metropolis is to raise questions about the suburban religious success. The churches would like to possess an authenticity apart from their particular engagement with man and his world, but there is no authentic church apart from this engagement. The Church is inseparable from her being in the world, for she is God's being for man in the world. The Church is only Church as she images, witnesses to and embodies that New Creation among men which is this being of God with man.

How tragic that in this truly eschatological stage of Western history the churches should turn from the eschatological reality to a sham religiousness in suburbia. This one truth of the New Creation then eludes them and they deceive those who turn to them for sanction and validation; they miss the truth that we cannot possess the future—the truth that the future is ours only in risking the relationships and position which we possess in the name of that community to which we belong in Christ—the New Mankind. Historical responsibility is exercised only in the courage of this kind of risk; hence, historical responsibility finds its source in the gift of a future, in the promise of meaning. The suburban dream of fulfillment is the illusion that we can possess the future, control it, limit its membership and finally take our ease within it. The promise of the holy city is the recognition that He who summons us was with us from the beginning;

[143]

whatever shattering separations the Future may hold, He who was with us in the beginning will continue with us.

We have spoken throughout in terms of an historical futurity in which men will find occasion to exercise their freedom and love in public life. We all know, nevertheless, that this way of speaking is qualified by the threat of a war which will cancel the significance of public life. This is not said with any intent to exaggerate the already existent eschatological orientation of our world. The threat of nuclear war only brings home to us our essentially human condition; we are those who live responsibly toward the future as that to which we belong and which we are called to appropriate through our own decisions in the present. The future is ours. However, the nuclear threat also makes eminently clear the public sphere in which the Church is called to focus her apostolate. The problem of nuclear threat is that men and women rush precipitately into an attempt to control their future, to possess it and remove its anxieties. This is the danger of the nuclear balance of terror, for it may lead at any moment to a headlong rush toward the future rather than a reflective participation in the authentic future of humanity. No one can seriously face this threat without fear, and yet no one can live authentically in the sphere of historical responsibility who has not received the courage to entertain that fear. The apostolate of reflection is not an activity apart from such considerations of the threat to humanity; this apostolate is the presence of the New Creation as courage to reflect in the midst of the threats to public life. The ministry of communication is not simply a private affair in some suburban neighborhood, although it may well include residential communities; this ministry is the recognition and response in which men and women discover their true responsibility for one another and through which public office becomes the responsible expression of human hope.

Men in public office have come to fear the intervention of the churches, for religious bodies so often step into the public arena in order to pursue their private advantage, whether this advantage be the maintenance of a blue law or the solicitation of funds for their private schools. A democratic society desperately needs a Church which can participate in its public life without acting as a faction in search of private advantage. Our society needs a ministry of laity. Our traditional religious structures are simply inappropriate for a democratic society with a pluralistic religious commitment. The days of the establishment are past. The Church will find its ministry of public responsibility through an apostolate of the laity and a ministry of servanthood in the structures of public life. This is her mission and opportunity in the emerging metropolis, but she cannot belong to this future and share in this ministry without the loss of her traditional structures and their false security.

Notes and Acknowledgments

These reflections are largely an attempt at theological construction in the field of metropolitan mission; consequently, a deliberate attempt was made to avoid discussions of the variety of perspectives that are emerging on this subject. Nevertheless, theological construction has grounds in a tradition and in the dialogue among fellow workers in the Church. The following comments acknowledge some of these shared understandings. Specific sources may, of course, be of interest to readers who would like to pursue particular questions, and for this reason they are included. Associates in the development of the Urban Training Center in Chicago, particularly Walter Kloetzli and Don Benedict, have contributed much informally to these reflections; it is our common hope that many of the concerns in these discussions will be pursued in this new center for metropolitan mission. In addition, discussions with the faculty of The Divinity School, University of Chicago, illuminated many points.

Chapter One: THE CALL TO SERVANTHOOD

The studies of Max Weber and Ernst Troeltsch provide a background for many of the problems considered throughout these chapters. Although the perspectives of these men have been shelved by their successors, the concern with social and historical relations of the churches in the world have continued to be the crucial issue for the contemporary Church; their pioneering work, not to mention their hypotheses and insights, play an incalculable role throughout these constructive considerations.

The considerations presented by E. C. Wickham in his monograph, *Church and People in an Industrial City*, continue to stimulate and provoke those who are concerned with the mission of the Church in an industrial world. The same can be said for Hendrik Kraemer's *A Theology of the Laity*. More recently, Francis O. Ayres of Parishfield has published a study on the Christian style of life under the title, *The Ministry of the Laity;* this analysis of Christian life and witness in contemporary society brings home very incisively the importance of training for the lay apostolate in the contemporary church. The author shares with Francis Ayres the conviction that the churches in the United States do not accept a serious ministry of the laity.

In a somewhat different vein, the study by Arthur J. Vidich and Joseph Bensman, *Small Town in Mass Society*, makes a significant contribution to our understanding of the emergence of our new social environment. W. Lloyd Warner's more recent researches on the emerging society have also been helpful, and particularly his summary lectures in *The Corporation in the Emergent American Society*. There is a developing literature on the mass society, but much of this awareness has been

Notes and Acknowledgments

missing in public and religious discussion. The author is also indebted to Dr. Hans Thimme for introducing him to the discussion of this subject by Dietrich von Oppen in his work *Das Personale Zeitalter*. Several recent papers on this theme deserve special acknowledgment: William L. C. Wheaton, "The Two Cultures and the Urban Revolution," a paper delivered at The National Conference on Urban Life, Washington, D.C., March 29, 1962; William Stringfellow, "The Mission of the Church in the Decadent Society," *Episcopal Theological School Journal*, Vol. VII, No. 1; Howard Moody, "The City: Necropolis or New Jerusalem," *Christianity and Crisis*, Vol. XXII, No. 15, Sept. 17, 1962. Furthermore, the World Council of Churches has initiated discussions of some of these problems under the ambiguous title of "The Missionary Structure of the Congregation." These discussions promise a new look at the problem of mission in an organizational society, and the author is particularly indebted to Pfarrer Werner Simpfendörfer of Bad Boll, Germany, for an opportunity to compare notes on these problems.

Chapter Two: THE SERVANT CHURCH IN A SECULARIZED WORLD

Several works have contributed to the clarification of the idea of secularization, even though these works represent divergent interpretations. Special reference can be made to the discussion of this theme in the following works: Helmut Thielicke, *Theologische Ethik*, Vol. I; Karl Holl, *The Cultural Significance of the Reformation;* Martin Stallmann, *Was Ist Säkularisierung?* (J. C. B. Mohr, Tübingen); H. H. Walz, "Christendom in a Secularized World," *The Ecumenical Review*, X, No. 3, April, 1958; Dietrich Bonhoeffer, *Prisoner for God;* Roger

Mehl, *La Sécularisation de la cité*, (Presses Universitaires de France); in addition to these more specific studies, a special debt is owed to the thoughtful consideration of the broader problems of freedom and humanity in Ernst Michel's book, *Der Partner Gottes* (Heidelberg, 1946).

Here again the discussions in the World Council of Churches have set in relief certain aspects of the Christian reality. The notion of the servant Church owes much to these World Council discussions. The preceding consideration of the Church in the emerging society is not an attempt to construct a utopia but an effort to delineate the figure of the authentic Church as it emerges in the contemporary world. Certain writers may anticipate this development or capture its essential themes in their reflections, but the work of reflection is to unfold the inner meaning of the authentic Church as we are given to share in it.

Chapter Three: THE PROPHETIC FELLOWSHIP

The development of the notion of reflection owes most to the thought of Gabriel Marcel, particularly his works, *The Mystery of Being* and *The Philosophy of Existence*. The work of Pierre Thévenaz, especially his *L'Homme et sa raison*, has been very illuminating with regard to the problem of history; the works of R. G. Collingwood, especially *The Idea of Nature* and *The Idea of History*, have been of considerable help. In this connection, the monograph by R. B. Y. Scott on *The Relevance of the Prophets* is extremely important for our contemporary understanding of the work of proclamation. Against the background of Gerhard Von Rad's interpretation of history in his *Old Testament Theology*, Vol. I., the notion of the prophetic fellowship emerges as the concrete expression of the New Creation in a secularized world.

The author is particularly indebted to the anonymous layman who wrote the letter from which an excerpt has been used; this layman is anonymous because the letter was shared by a clergyman whose name is now lost to the author's memory. This layman's letter can be matched with statements and letters by many other laymen, but there is a directness in the statement of the enclosed citation which clarifies the real issue confronting the churches in their task of proclamation. It is ironical that the clergy often hesitate over the apostolate of the laity on the ground of the theological ineptitude of laymen, and yet much of the real theological insight of our time is coming directly from lay witness.

Chapter Four: THE MINISTRY OF COMMUNICATION

The particular themes of the interpersonal world and the significance of recognition have found much more attention in the European than the American literature. The works of Paul Ricœur, Maurice Merleau-Ponty and Gabriel Marcel are certainly the most prominent for the author; however, Roger Mehl's *Rencontre d'autrui* is a profound treatment of this theme. The author also owes a considerable debt to William Poteat whose unpublished lectures some years ago on the "Metaphor of I and Thou" were especially helpful in clarifying the theological significance of the interpersonal.

On the more practical side, the work of the Detroit Industrial Mission continues to play a crucial role in the author's thought on the new form of the Church in an organizational society. The reports of the mission staff and conversations with them have been decisive in guiding these thoughts on the servanthood of the laity. The same can be said for the work of Robert L. Green in the Ecumenical Center in Wilton, Connecticut. The report of that center indicates both the problems and the possibilities of a ministry that moves into the arena of public life. It is evident in this center that suburbia is not a geographical but a mental reality, and the mind of suburbia can as well be found in the middle of the city, as the openness of the New Mankind may be evoked in a suburban center. The center in Wilton has countered the retreat to privacy with a summons to involvement in public responsibility.

In the concluding remarks the author is indebted to Jaroslav Pelikan for suggestions on the theme of the city and to Albert T. Mollegen for his discussions of the relationship of amnesia to *anamnesis* in a different connection. Opportunities to discuss all of these problems have been provided by the Human Relations Council of Houston, Texas, the Board of Social action of The United Church of Christ, the American Association of Theological Schools and others; each of these situations has opened new insight on the problems.